New Directions for
Higher Education

Martin Kramer and
Betsy Barefoot
CO-EDITORS-IN-CHIEF

Multinational Colleges and Universities: Leading, Governing, and Managing International Branch Campuses

Jason E. Lane
Kevin Kinser
EDITORS

Number 155 • Fall 2011
Jossey-Bass
San Francisco

MULTINATIONAL COLLEGES AND UNIVESITIES: LEADING, GOVERNING, AND MANAGING INTERNATIONAL BRANCH CAMPUSES
Jason E. Lane, Kevin Kinser
New Directions for Higher Education, no. 155
Martin Kramer, Betsy Barefoot, Co-Editors-in-Chief

Copyright © 2011 Wiley Periodicals, Inc., A Wiley Company. All rights reserved. No part of this publication may be reproduced in any form or by any means, except as permitted under sections 107 and 108 of the 1976 United States Copyright Act, without either the prior written permission of the publisher or authorization through the Copyright Clearance Center, 222 Rosewood Drive, Danvers, MA 01923; (978) 750-8400; fax (978) 646-8600. The copyright notice appearing at the bottom of the first page of a chapter in this journal indicates the copyright holder's consent that copies may be made for personal or internal use, or for personal or internal use of specific clients, on the condition that the copier pay for copying beyond that permitted by law. This consent does not extend to other kinds of copying, such as copying for general distribution, for advertising or promotional purposes, for creating collective works, or for resale. Such permission requests and other permission inquiries should be addressed to the Permissions Department, c/o John Wiley & Sons, Inc., 111 River Street, Hoboken, NJ 07030; (201) 748-6011; fax (201) 748-6008; www.wiley.com/go/permissions.

Microfilm copies of issues and articles are available in 16mm and 35mm, as well as microfiche in 105mm, through University Microfilms Inc., 300 North Zeeb Road, Ann Arbor, MI 48106-1346.

NEW DIRECTIONS FOR HIGHER EDUCATION (ISSN 0271-0560, electronic ISSN 1536-0741) is part of The Jossey-Bass Higher and Adult Education Series and is published quarterly by Wiley Subscription Services, Inc., A Wiley Company, at Jossey-Bass, 989 Market Street, San Francisco, CA 94103-1741. Periodicals Postage Paid at San Francisco, California, and at additional mailing offices. POSTMASTER: Send address changes to New Directions for Higher Education, Jossey-Bass, 989 Market Street, San Francisco, CA 94103-1741.

New Directions for Higher Education is indexed in Current Index to Journals in Education (ERIC); Higher Education Abstracts.

SUBSCRIPTIONS cost $89 for individuals and $275 for institutions, agencies, and libraries. See ordering information page at end of journal.

EDITORIAL CORRESPONDENCE should be sent to the Co-Editors-in-Chief, Martin Kramer, 2807 Shasta Road, Berkeley, CA 94708-2011 and Betsy Barefoot, Gardner Institute, Box 72, Brevard, NC 28712.

Cover photograph © Digital Vision

www.josseybass.com

CONTENTS

EDITORS' NOTES   1
Jason E. Lane, Kevin Kinser

1. Global Expansion of International Branch Campuses: Managerial and Leadership Challenges   5
Jason E. Lane
This chapter outlines the growth of IBCs over the past fifty years and discusses some of the major management and leadership challenges associated with creating and sustaining IBCs.

2. Strategies for Managing and Leading an Academic Staff in Multiple Countries   19
Rebecca Hughes
Faculty are a critical component to the success of the academic branch campus. In an environment where academic quality is constantly in question, the management and leadership of the academic staff are important, particularly when that staff is spread across multiple geographic locations.

3. Institutional Ethos: Replicating the Student Experience   29
Cynthia Howman Wood
A common criticism of IBCs is that they cannot recreate the student culture of the home campus. While this is true, some IBCs have gone to great lengths to not only create a comparable culture for their students, but also to integrate their students into the culture of the home campus.

4. Identifying Fit of Mission and Environment: Applying the American Community College Model Internationally   41
Mary S. Spangler, Arthur Q. Tyler Jr.
This chapter discusses the exporting of the American community college model and the importance of identifying a good "fit" with local partners.

5. Multinational Quality Assurance   53
Kevin Kinser
This chapter highlights the dilemmas facing traditional models of quality assurance in a global environment where higher education institutions can and do cross geopolitical borders.

6. Operational Considerations for Opening a Branch Campus Abroad 65

Lawrence M. Harding, Robert W. Lammey

This chapter provides specific advice for how IBCs can negotiate entry into a foreign legal environment and operate support systems that can coordinate the management operations on multiple campuses.

7. The Cross-Border Education Policy Context: Educational Hubs, Trade Liberalization, and National Sovereignty 79

Jason E. Lane, Kevin Kinser

Policies for importing and exporting international branch campuses are increasingly being formalized, with a number of countries explicitly encouraging educational trade as an economic development goal.

8. Selected Resources and Bibliography 87

Cross-Border Education Research Team (C-BERT)

This chapter provides an annotated bibliography of resources pertaining to IBCs.

INDEX 109

EDITORS' NOTES

International branch campuses (IBCs) are part of the leading edge of development in the global higher education sector. Internally, they are part of the transformation of some higher education institutions into multinational enterprises, operating campuses, offices, and research sites around the globe. Externally, they are part of a growing trend of governments relying on foreign education providers to build their local education capacity and to garner increased international attention. Over the past decade, IBCs have been the target of much criticism (some deserved, some not) and a little praise (mostly from those intimately involved with their operations). However, scholarly writing about the topic has been limited, though it has increased precipitously in the past five years. We see the role of this volume as using the extant scholarly literature, original research, and observations from experts to provide readers with insights about the practice of leading IBCs.

Unlike most other developments in higher education, IBCs are a global phenomenon. They transcend national boundaries, and the study of such institutions cannot be limited to any one national context. As McBurnie and Zyguris (2007, 6–7) note in their book about transnational education, because most research on globalization in higher education is conducted from a national perspective, institutions are more often portrayed as victims rather than protagonists in developing strategies to succeed on a global scale.

This focus on the national context has also limited inquiry into the development of multinational colleges and universities. The study of multinational colleges and universities and their offspring, the international branch campus, requires a global perspective.

This volume arose out of the long-standing interest of the volume's editors in understanding the emergence of multinational educational institutions. These interests fostered the development of the Cross-Border Education Research Team (C-BERT), which provided the scholarly foundation for this volume. C-BERT is a collaborative project led by professors Kevin Kinser and Jason Lane of the Institute for Global Education Policy Studies at the University at Albany, State University of New York. The team is comprised of six graduate assistants in the University's department of Educational Administration and Policy Studies (www.albany.edu/eaps). The team includes Jill Crombie Borgos, Tom Enderlein, Christine Farrugia, Dan Knox, David Phillips, and Linda Tsevi. Together, they have dedicated much effort over the past year tracking various IBC developments and creating an extensive annotated bibliography, a sample of which is included at the end of this volume.

C-BERT tracks the development and movement of educational institutions crossing borders through the use of site visits, interviews with policy

NEW DIRECTIONS FOR HIGHER EDUCATION, no. 155, Fall 2011 © Wiley Periodicals, Inc.
Published online in Wiley Online Library (wileyonlinelibrary.com) • DOI:10.1002/he.439

2 MULTINATIONAL COLLEGES AND UNIVERSITIES

makers and academic leaders, review of literature, and analysis of media reports. The C-BERT team members have visited nearly 50 home and branch campuses of multinational colleges and universities spread across 15 countries in Asia, Australia, Europe, the Middle East, and North America. Much of the research developed by C-BERT, as well as part of our annotated bibliography, is available on the web site www.globalhighered.org. Like this volume, the intended audience of the web site is both scholars and practitioners. The C-BERT web site is dedicated to providing research and media updates about the development of multinational colleges and universities around the globe. Information available on the site includes an up-to-date list of international branch campuses (including those that have closed), summary description of locations that have stated a desire to become an educational hub, an annotated bibliography of relevant literature, and weekly updates of media clippings about IBCs and other institutional movements across borders.

This particular volume is dedicated to the hundreds of practitioners who work at IBCs. As discussed throughout the various chapters, those leading and working at IBCs face challenges unlike those confronted by their colleagues on the home campus. Not only do these individuals face unique environmental conditions; they also have to find ways to balance local demands with the expectations of the home campus. While their experiences may differ from those on the home campus, they do share much with others working at IBCs. Yet, there are few formal means through which those working at IBCs can discuss their shared challenges and learn from each other.

In a recent chapter about the global outreach of Carnegie Mellon University, Mark Kamlet (2010), the institution's president, laments that "surely there should be some mechanism of forum by which we can all share our experiences [in creating multinational institutions]. Each of us inventing or reinventing the wheel on many of these logistics is . . . not a very appealing way to proceed" (p. 85). In this volume we attempt to take up this challenge, to provide a modest forum for scholars and practitioners to discuss some of the challenges confronted by the many faculty and staff who work at these international outposts.

The volume is designed to provide readers with an overview of the IBC phenomenon, as well as provide practical insights from those directly involved in the development of multinational colleges and universities. We begin with an overview of the development of IBCs. The first chapter, by Jason Lane, traces the history of such institutions and discusses the various intentions behind their creation and the roles they play in the host country. The chapter also provides an overview of some of the key challenges faced by those leading and managing IBCs.

The next two chapters deal specifically with issues pertaining to faculty and students. Chapter 2 focuses on strategies for managing and leading academic staff spread across multiple countries. The author, Rebecca Hughes, is the Pro Vice-Chancellor for Internationalization at the University of Sheffield in the United Kingdom. Before assuming this role, Professor Hughes was Chair of Applied Linguistics at the University of Nottingham and led the development of the University's English for Academic Purposes program, which was spread across campuses in China, Malaysia, and the United Kingdom. The third chapter looks at the challenges of replicating the student collegiate experience that exists on the home campus. Cynthia Howman Wood, Director of Student Activities at Texas A&M Qatar, discusses the importance of facilitating the creation of a student culture in the IBC and uses examples from Texas A&M to illustrate challenges that can arise when trying to replicate the student culture on the home campus in a distant location.

The challenges that are confronted by IBC leaders are not constrained to internal structures and practices. In chapter 4, Mary Spangler and Arthur Tyler Jr., both of Houston Community College (HCC), discuss the increasing interest among developing nations to create a community college system similar to that in the United States. The authors point out that many developing nations do not have two-year institutions, yet there is a growing need for more high-skilled vocational training to support increasing demands in the workforce. Spangler and Tyler discuss HCC's expansion into several other countries and their belief that their growing global engagements are an extension of the traditional service mission of the community colleges.

The final three chapters focus on the regulatory, legal, and policy environments. In chapter 5, Kevin Kinser highlights the dilemmas facing the traditional models of quality assurance as institutions begin to move across borders. Kinser provides an overview of how home and host countries are working to adapt their quality assurance practices to fit the characteristics of multinational educational institutions. In chapter 6, Lawrence Harding and Robert Lammey provide in-depth instructions to institutions about how to adapt business operations to deal with the challenges dealing with dual operating expectations, tax issues, and labor laws. The authors draw on their extensive experience helping many types of organizations establish and operate presences in other countries. Finally, in chapter 7, Jason Lane and Kevin Kinser discuss the emerging policy issues surrounding the development of IBCs, in particular focusing on the development strategies of nations looking to become educational hubs.

At the end of the volume, readers will find an extensive annotated bibliography of nearly a hundred scholarly and policy writings that deal directly with international branch campuses. This bibliography is divided into several sections to help readers navigate the extensive listing. The sections include: General, Arab Gulf, Asia, Development Perspective, Management, Quality, Students, Teaching and Learning, and Trade and Regulation. Each reading is listed only once, though many could be classified under multiple sections.

In assembling this volume, we have become even more aware of both the challenges and opportunities associated with international branch campuses.

4 MULTINATIONAL COLLEGES AND UNIVERSITIES

Their too common existence on the periphery of home campuses' organizational operations can threaten the sustainability of the IBC as well as risk the reputation of the home campus. However, many IBCs are organizations of substance, providing quality academic programs and engaging in research and service that is relevant and important for the communities in which they reside. This volume is intended to make accessible information about what is already known in terms of leadership, administration, and governance of IBCs and to draw on the lessons learned from the field. Yet, there remains a clear need for additional scholarship in this area.

Jason E. Lane
Kevin Kinser
Editors

References

Kamlet, M. 2010. "Offering Domestic Degrees Outside the United States: One University's Experiences Over the Past Decade." In *Higher Education in a Global Society*, edited by B. Johnstone and M. B. d'Ambrosio, 83–107. Cheltenham, UK: Edward Elgar.

McBurnie, G., and C. Ziguras. 2007. *Transnational Education: Issues and Trends in Offshore Higher Education*. New York: Routledge.

JASON E. LANE is an Assistant Professor, Senior Researcher at the Institute for Global Education Policy Studies, and Senior Fellow at the Rockefeller Institute of Government, State University of New York, Albany. He co-leads the Cross-Border Education Research Team (www.globalhighered.org).

KEVIN KINSER is an Associate Professor, Senior Researcher at the Institute for Global Education Policy Studies, State University of New York, Albany. He co-leads the Cross-Border Education Research Team (www.globalhighered.org).

This chapter outlines the growth of IBCs over the past fifty years and discusses some of the major management and leadership challenges associated with creating and sustaining IBCs.

Global Expansion of International Branch Campuses: Managerial and Leadership Challenges

Jason E. Lane

Introduction

In his book *The World Is Flat* (2005), Thomas Friedman effectively argued that globalization has led to the creation of worldwide markets and a leveling of the playing field for the competitors within those markets. Higher education has not escaped this trend. The last decade has witnessed the development of multinational colleges and universities: institutions that have extended their academic operations outside of their home country with a combination of research sites, outreach offices, joint degree programs, and branch campuses. The development of such multinational educational enterprises requires an academic leader who can balance the requirements of the home country with the demands of the host environment, operate in multiple cultures almost simultaneously, and have the capacity to deal with the ambiguities and challenges associated with start-up ventures.

This chapter introduces the volume's focus on leading, managing, and governing international branch campuses (IBCs). An IBC is a very specific type of international activity through which an institution in one country, referred to as the *home* country, opens a campus in another country, or the *host* country. For the purposes of this volume, an international branch campus is defined as an entity that is owned, at least in part, by a foreign education provider; operated in the name of the foreign education provider; engages in at least some face-to-face teaching; and provides access to an entire academic program that leads to a credential awarded by the foreign education provider. Because of the complexity involved in establishing and

6   MULTINATIONAL COLLEGES AND UNIVERSITIES

operating IBCs, the governance and management of these institutions can be very different from that of the home campus.

Readers are provided with an introduction to the IBC phenomenon, including an overview of the growth of IBCs as well as the challenges facing IBC leaders. Part one of the chapter provides a discussion of the global expansion of IBCs. The second part focuses on the motivations for opening a branch campus and the roles they play in the local environment, with parts three and four explaining some of the conditions of the local environment and the cultural impact. The chapter then describes the types of boundaries with which IBC leaders may have to deal and concludes with an overview of issues for future investigation. In addition to a review of secondary sources, the chapter primarily draws upon data gathered by the Cross-Border Education Research Team (C-BERT) at the University at Albany, State University of New York. C-BERT has conducted extensive research into the development of IBCs, including a compilation of bibliographic materials, interviews with dozens of campus leaders, and site visits to more than fifty IBCs in ten countries. Unless otherwise cited, the information provided in this chapter is drawn directly from this extensive data set.

The Global Growth of IBCs

Available records suggest that a campus in Italy opened by Johns Hopkins in the 1950s in order to provide graduate programs in international relations may be the oldest IBC in continuous existence to operate on foreign land (Verbik and Merkley 2006). However, Florida State and several other institutions have been providing programs outside of the US borders since at least 1933 in order to serve US military and civilian personnel located in the US-owned Canal Zone. The Florida State presence formally converted into an IBC in Panama after the Panamanians took over the Zone in 1999. Further development of IBCs came slowly. In the 1970s, at least five additional IBCs were opened. They were all American-based institutions, and the IBCs were located in Mexico (Aliant International University), Belgium (Boston University), United Kingdom (American Intercontinental University), Greece (University of La Verne), and Switzerland (Webster University)(Becker 2009).

During the 1980s, the first concentrated buildup of IBCs in one country occurred in Japan (Chambers and Cummings 1990). Japanese leaders wanted to further strengthen the country's relationship with the United States, and actively recruited several American universities to establish branch campuses in the country. In the United States, many academic leaders wanted to take advantage of having a presence in one of the fastest-growing economies in the world. However, while at least 30 American institutions established IBCs in Japan during the 1980s, only Temple University remains today. The bursting of this IBC bubble was brought on by instability in the local economy, which stagnated after the 1980s; the difficulty in finding

Table 1.1. Number of IBCs by Geographic Region Where IBC Is Located

Africa	Asia	Australia/ Oceania	Caribbean/ Central America	Europe	Middle East	North America	South America
7	53	5	9	36	56	13	4

Source: C-BERT, 2011

students able to engage in English language instruction; and poor choice of campus locations, which were mainly in areas difficult to travel to outside of the city (Chambers and Cummings 1990).

A second phase of growth began in the 1990s, when diversification of both home and host countries began. In 1990, French Fashion University Esmod opened a campus in Norway, which may have been the first non-American institution to open an IBC. During this decade, educational institutions from countries such as Australia, Mexico, Chile, Ireland, Canada, Italy, the United Kingdom, and Sweden began opening campuses abroad. The destination of such campuses expanded beyond the developed world to Africa, Asia, the Middle East, and South America. By the end of the 1990s, approximately fifty IBCs had been established, not including those that were part of the 1980s' Japanese bubble.

By 2011, the number of IBCs grew to 183 worldwide (C-BERT, 2011).[1] These institutions are now located on every inhabitable continent (see Table 1.1). Nearly half of all IBCs are part of an institution in the United States, with Australia and the United Kingdom being the other significant exporters. Most of the IBCs are now located in Asia and the Middle East, with nearly a third in the United Arab Emirates. Moreover, there are at least 13 countries that both import and export IBCs. Australia, the United Kingdom, and the United States all host a few IBCs, though they export many more than they host. Others that both import and export institutions are Canada, Malaysia, Belgium, France, Italy, Mexico, the Netherlands, Russia, South Korea, and Switzerland.

Purposes and Roles of IBCs

This section focuses specifically on the reasons why institutions may choose to expand into a foreign country and the roles that they may play in the host country. Chapter 7 in this volume provides further discussion about the policy dynamics of the host and home countries that influence the development of IBCs. It is important for the leaders of IBCs to realize not only the intentions of the home campus for authorizing the creation of the IBC, but also the role that such institutions can play in the host country. Often these roles do not meet with traditional conceptions of the role of private higher education providers, which is the standard classification of IBCs.

8   Multinational Colleges and Universities

Though there has been no systematic investigation of institutional motivations to open an IBC, the most common reasons cited in the literature are the desire for new revenue streams, the pursuit of increased institutional prestige, and the belief that such international engagements will improve the educational quality of the institution (e.g., Becker 2009; Eckel, Green, and Berniaz in press; McBurnie and Ziguras 2007; Naidoo 2010; Rizvi 2004; Verbik and Merkley 2006). Regardless of the stated priority of revenue generation, the pursuit of monetary resources is particularly salient, as most IBCs are intended to be self-supporting entities. Whether by government restrictions or institutional choice, most IBCs are not subsidized by the home institution, and many hope to generate sufficient revenue to support activities on the home campus. The three primary sources of new financial support are tuition, host government subsidy, and private partner investment.

The actual role of IBCs within the host country is also little examined. Lane (2011) evaluated the IBCs in Dubai and Malaysia following Levy's (1986) typology of purposes of private higher education. Lane (2011) found that IBCs matched Levy's model, which suggests that private higher education develops in order to 1) provide something different from what is already provided; 2) provide something better than is provided; or 3) absorb excess demand in the system. In the case of Malaysia and Dubai, some IBCs provide access to different academic programs, different teaching styles, or a different type of educational experience (e.g., British or Indian) than provided elsewhere in the country. Further, these IBCs, while not always extensions of the most prestigious institutions, mostly come from nations with a well-respected and highly sought after higher education sector (e.g., United States, United Kingdom, and Australia). Thus, some were viewed as "better quality" options than otherwise available within the host country. Finally, the IBCs in the study were part of a supply-side government strategy. That is, instead of meeting excess demand for higher education, the presence of IBCs was intended to create new demand in the local higher education sector, keeping local students from studying abroad and attracting foreign students to come study within the host country.

Moreover, while the institutions engage in certain roles similar to other private higher education entities, they also share certain characteristics with public institutions. IBCs are almost exclusively viewed as part of the privatization trend in higher education. However, many such institutions fulfill a public mission within the host country (McBurnie 2002; Trani and Holsworth 2010). For example, Lane and Kinser (2011) found that in some nations, IBCs receive a great deal of financial support from the local government and are intended to fulfill public goals such as providing access to local students and engaging in service to the local community. As pointed out in their article, in certain cases there is even a higher expectation of engaging in the local community for the faculty on the branch campus than at the home campus.

Understanding Local Conditions

The local environment in which the IBC operates is often very different from that of the home campus (Debowski 2005; Fegan and Field 2009; Vinen and Selvarajah 2008). As social organizations, it is the nature of colleges and universities to adapt to their local environmental conditions. Their policies, practices, and structures are designed to take advantage of the local legal, cultural, and economic conditions (Lane and Kinser 2008). However, IBCs are often located in environments that are very different from that of the home campus. Thus, the practices that proved successful for the home campus in dealing with its environment have not always proven successful for the IBC's interaction with its local environment.

Leaders of IBCs need to understand how local conditions differ from that of the home campus and find ways to adapt existing policies and practices to best meet those different demands, while still respecting the standards and ethos of the home campus. An example is that of the recruitment process, which is particularly salient given the reliance of many IBCs on tuition revenue. First, the college choice process of students in the host country is often very different from those in the home country. Leaders of American IBCs in the Middle East have reported that a vast majority of students only begin to show interest in an institution a month or two prior to the start of the fall semester, and many show up the first week of classes expecting to be admitted. This is very different from students in America, who usually begin planning for college several years in advance of their admittance, applying up to a year in advance. Second, many applicants have not taken the necessary standardized exams required by many colleges and universities; nor do they have sufficient language skills that would allow them to be successful in an advanced course of study (the language of instruction for most IBCs is English). Third, regardless of the international reputation of an institution, an IBC must compete locally. This often means establishing a local brand recognition and learning to differentiate from local competitors, most of whom the home campus would never have considered as competitors. Many IBCs rarely understand these issues until after they have already set up shop, and it is often very difficult for the home campus administrators to understand these issues from afar. To address the issue, IBC leaders need to work with the home campus to adapt institutional policies to allow for local conditions, but also maintain the quality standards of the home campus. In some cases, institutions have created special "academies" to educate students with sub-par qualifications in English and other areas. Participation in these academies does not guarantee admission to the university, but they can help prepare students for admission and serve as potential enrollment pipelines for the IBC.

Despite the differences between the home and host environments, many home campuses do not allow IBCs much freedom to adapt their policies and

10   MULTINATIONAL COLLEGES AND UNIVERSITIES

procedures to local conditions. This often seems to come from a fear that adaptation would lessen quality and negatively affect the home campus reputation. Since the IBC operates in the name of the home campus, there is a need to ensure that academic programs are of comparable quality. However, administrative functions that support the academic activities of the branch could be viewed more flexibly in light of unique local conditions. Of particular concern is administrative protocols being controlled by managers on the home campus. In one case, for example, IBC admissions were handled centrally by the home campus under identical procedures and review processes. Not adapting the recruitment and procedures to the host country environment made it difficult for admissions staff to recruit students and led to students feeling frustrated by the process, ultimately to the detriment of IBC's success.

IBC leaders need to be sure to engage in due diligence in advance of creating the IBC or of accepting the leadership position. In many cases, those making the decisions about whether to open an IBC in a particular country have relied primarily on a limited number of contacts in the host country. Ample evidence from the literature and C-BERT documentation suggests that academic leaders are not fully vetting their intended foreign partners or the information that they provide. Moreover, academic leaders seem to make decisions based on extrapolations of knowledge about the home institution environment without fully investigating host country environmental conditions.

According to C-BERT data, most IBCs that have closed their doors have done so because they failed to adapt to the local environment or their business plans were flawed or based on inaccurate or unsubstantiated data. In both failed and successful IBCs, enrollment projections usually fall short and the academic preparation of students proves to be lower than what is initially assumed. Degrees desired by government or other local employers may not necessarily translate into student interest in those degree programs—a substantial dilemma for a tuition-driven financial model. Thus, IBCs need to be certain to offer degrees that local students have an interest in pursuing. In practice, this often means that an IBC's academic programs are mostly professionally oriented, such as business and engineering (see, e.g., Lane 2010b for a discussion of degree offerings in Dubai). With time, however, some institutions have expanded their academic offering to include lower-demand programs, such as the humanities and social sciences, once a local reputation is established and the IBC has sufficient enrollments to allow for cross-subsidization of academic programs.

While it is important for IBC leaders to understand the need to adapt to local conditions, they also need to be aware of the stability or fragility of the local environment. Most IBCs are located in developing nations, where both governments and the higher education sectors may be in flux. Few institutions would make a decision to open an IBC in a country where they think the government may be overturned; however, the events of early 2011

GLOBAL EXPANSION OF IBCS: MANAGERIAL AND LEADERSHIP CHALLENGES   11

in Egypt and some other Arab countries show that it is not always possible to predict the stability of a nation. Even when a government is stable, most IBCs are operating in very fluid higher education sectors. Altbach (2010) has suggested that the expansion of the local higher education sector may prove to be one of the most significant threats to the sustainability of IBCs. In extreme cases, McBurnie and Ziguras (2007) have suggested that it would even be possible for host governments to nationalize IBCs and incorporate them into the local public sector, though no country has yet to do so. These potential concerns reinforce the fact that even though some educational institutions are becoming multinational, education remains locally embedded.

The Cultural Impact

The cultural issues that exist can be vast and complicated. Culture can affect operational issues ranging from pedagogical practice to the purchase of computers to student housing. Most of the research in this area has focused on issues pertaining to teaching. Indeed, faculty can face significant challenges when teaching students with different linguistic and cultural backgrounds (Bodycott and Walker 2000) or with different learning styles (Rostron 2009), particularly when teaching involves the use of translators (Debowski 2005). Such difficulties have become particularly obvious when an institution from a Western country opens in a non-Western country.[2] For example, Rostron (2009) notes the tension that exists between the liberal arts perspective of Western higher education and the expectations of Qataris for transnational providers in their country. Qatar education has historically been related to religious instruction and its modern roots lie in an oral tradition, memorization, and transmission of knowledge. Culturally, Rostron suggests, students may have difficulty with Western expectations of dialogue, active learning, and critical thinking.

Culture also affects the development of student activities, residence halls, and other cocurricular experiences. Many host countries are much more conservative in nature than the home country, and it is important that the IBC leadership and staff understand different cultural traditions and expectations. For example, in many Islamic countries, it is not appropriate (and in some places illegal) for unrelated men and women to reside together. Thus, it is important to have student residence halls with a clear demarcation between where male and female students live, even if the students are not Muslim. Further, certain traditions or customs that are used on the home campus may not translate to the home campus. In chapter 3, Howman Wood discusses how Texas A&M could not use their mascot, a dog named Reveille, at their Qatar campus. Many Arab societies, including those in Qatar, view dogs as feral beasts and bad omens. Importantly, the religious and cultural customs of some nations may require respect and some level of adherence even if the students or staff are not members of that religion or culture. In many Islamic cultures, non-Muslims do not have to abide

12 MULTINATIONAL COLLEGES AND UNIVERSITIES

by all religious rules; however, in some nations, there are certain expectations about how all men and women should dress and how non-Muslims should act during religious holidays. For example, while non-Muslim students would not be expected to fast all day during Ramadan, which is the requirement of Islam, many locations frown on anyone eating or drinking in public areas. Thus, during Ramadan, some campuses have designated certain rooms, usually without windows, as locations where non-Muslims can eat and drink during the day.

Finally, culture can affect basic business operations. Those in charge of IBCs have to deal with outfitting the campus space, obtaining information technology, and maintaining various support systems. On the home campus, there usually exist various support units with the responsibility for dealing with many of these procurement issues. The branch campus usually does not have such a support structure in place and cannot use the experts at the home campus, as most equipment and supplies have to be purchased locally. It is a truism that people do not shop in the same way in all countries; the concept of the contract does not directly translate across cultures. In fact, many IBCs are located in places where deals are done with haggling and a handshake, not bidding and contracts. For example, one interview participant at an IBC in the Middle East talked about a particularly frustrating information technology (IT) purchase.

> I worked for several weeks with a representative from [a local company] to identify the exact piece of computer equipment we needed and then to get it at a fair price. And this is not an inexpensive piece of equipment; we're talking a couple of hundred thousand dollars [USD]. So, we finally made the deal and got the contract written up. However, by the time I got approval from the home campus to go ahead with the deal, the person I was working with was gone and I had to start all over haggling with someone else.

In this and other stories from IBC staff, frustration stems from both inexperience in dealing with such situations and the inability of the home campus to understand that other countries will not always conform to their procedures.

Spanning Boundaries: Challenges for IBC Leaders

IBCs are filled with structural and cultural boundaries and successful IBC leaders must learn to overcome such boundaries. The liberalization of trade policies and improvement of technology have allowed for colleges and universities to overcome geographic boundaries and expand their global footprint, but little attention has been given to how these changes have affected the operational aspects of these multinational educational organizations. In some ways the ease of expansion has created more boundaries within the administrative and academic operations.

When spanning boundaries, individuals are often associated with each group that the boundary divides (Scott 2006). Unfortunately, the tendency is for neither group to claim the boundary spanner as one of its own. In fact, the boundary spanner will often be perceived as working on behalf of the other group and may encounter distrust from both groups. Despite these drawbacks, not learning to span the boundaries that are part of the IBC can risk the sustainability of the organization. The types of boundaries that exist within IBCs are briefly described next.

Campus Boundaries. The most significant boundary that exists is that between the home campus and the branch campus. No matter how the IBC is structured or how it is governed, those on the home campus usually view the IBC as part as something "different" or "apart" from the home campus. Coleman (2003) explains this phenomenon by suggesting that those on the home campus often consider the IBC within the institutional periphery and rarely consider it a part of the academic core. As such, it is often considered a low priority for many on the home campus. Lim's (2008) study of Australian IBCs illustrated the impact of such a boundary in finding that that there was a general lack of agreement between the home and branch in terms of what it meant to provide a comparable education to students. Lane's (2010a) analysis of governance structures found that faculty and staff on the IBC often feel disenfranchised and disconnected as they have limited means for engaging in the institutional governance structures. And Hefferman and Poole (2004), in their study of Australian universities in Southeast Asia, found that disconnects between the campuses can lead to an absence of trust, commitment, and effective communication, which can in turn lead to a deterioration of the offshore enterprise.

Vertical Boundaries. The creation of an IBC often merges, at least in terms of geographic proximity, several functions that operate distinctly from each other on the home campus. However, the vertical administrative silos that exist on the home campus can often be extended to the IBC. Many American IBCs in the Middle East use the same academic and administrative governance structures as exist at the home campus. These horizontal boundaries can make it difficult for those within the IBC to work as a team to operate the IBC. These vertical boundaries sometimes create further problems when the academic and professional staff report back to supervisors or departments on the home campus. This reporting structure may be intended to help integrate the IBC staff with counterparts on the home campus and to ensure compliance with home campus policies and procedures. Unfortunately, this can reestablish the home campus silos at the IBC and may make it difficult for the IBC leader to coordinate the functions of the IBC.

Temporal Boundaries. Many IBCs are located several time zones apart from the home campus. In many cases, there is very little overlap in the workdays of the two campuses, making it difficult to coordinate meetings and often extending the decision-making processes. This is particularly problematic when the IBC exists in a country when the workweek runs

14   MULTINATIONAL COLLEGES AND UNIVERSITIES

from Sunday through Thursday, as is often the case in majority Muslim countries where Friday is a holy day. The temporal boundary makes it difficult for even simple issues to be quickly addressed when it involves staff on both campuses. The time differential can make it difficult for individuals to discuss an issue over the phone or to quickly exchange e-mails and when meetings are scheduled. Furthermore, those making time-sensitive decisions on the home campus do not often think about the impact of their decisions on the functions of the IBC. For example, it is not unusual for IT administrators to schedule updates to student-management software in the middle of the night so as to minimize the impact on users. However, what is the middle of the night at the home campus may be the middle of the workday at the IBC and thus cause a severe disruption in services. IBC leaders must recognize the effect of temporal boundaries and find ways for the staff at both campuses to compromise on their schedules and help the home campus staff to realize the potential implications for their decisions on the functions of the IBC.

Future Issues

International branch campuses are part of an organizational ecology that is different from any other organizational type within the spectrum of educational organizations. They do not fit neatly within the organizational populations in either their home or host countries. Indeed, their population is global in nature, traversing national borders and student markets. Though they are spread across six continents, they share a number of management and leadership issues seemingly unique to their organization type.

This chapter presents some of the commonalities that exist among IBCs, providing a brief overview of the cross-border dynamics affecting their operations, as well as key management and leadership issues. However, these are not stagnant organizations. As an organizational population, they remain relatively young and they are likely to change at a faster rate than what their home campuses are likely to change. This chapter concludes with three issues that warrant future attention and study.

The Need for Comparative Data. No organization or agency has systematically collected data specifically about these institutions. Because of this, the history of the phenomenon is largely anecdotal. No one knows how many total students are enrolled or have graduated from these institutions. Nor is there information about where students come from or where they go after graduation. Similarly, no data exists about the number of faculty or staff or the qualifications of those individuals. What is known about IBCs has been collected as part of policy reports, institutional audits, interviews, and idiosyncratic case studies. And despite the amount of commentary that is beginning to emerge on the topic, there is no trend data on which to fully understand the current status or future of IBCs. An annual global survey of IBCs would allow a more complete understanding of this organizational population.

NEW DIRECTIONS FOR HIGHER EDUCATION • DOI:10.1002/he

GLOBAL EXPANSION OF IBCs: MANAGERIAL AND LEADERSHIP CHALLENGES   15

Development of Research Capacity. Started primarily as teaching institutions, a few have developed substantial research capacity, and a growing number of IBCs encourage their faculty to pursue a research agenda. These research agendas tend to be locally relevant and, at times, funded by local funds. It seems that the research programs are most prominent at locations where the host government has begun to provide funds to the IBC. For example, the campus of Georgia Institute of Technology (United States) in France runs a collaborative lab dealing with telecommunications and innovative materials that is partly funded by the French government. The University of Nottingham's (United Kingdom) campus in Malaysia received support from Malaysia's National Cancer Council to support research into potential anticancer drugs derived from Malaysian wildlife. However, many IBCs also now appear to be creating internal programs to help foster a research environment. The University of Wollongong-Dubai (UOWD; Australia) began offering a doctorate of business in 2010 and supporting its faculty to create research-based case studies relevant to the practice of business in the Middle East; UOWD also provides research seed-grants to faculty in other areas. Nearby, at the Dubai campus of the Middlesex University (United Kingdom), an interinstitutional research forum was designed to bring together researchers to share and collaborate on research. More research needs to be done regarding the growing research agendas and capacities within IBCs, but such developments suggest that these institutions are becoming more locally engaged in relevant research and could signal long-term commitment to the regions in which they are located.

Public Diplomacy Role. IBCs are not merely extensions of their home campus. For better or for worse, these institutions are often perceived as extensions of their home country. For example, in a set of interviews with students in the Middle East, some perceived the closure of a single IBC from the US as "America" pulling out of the region. Even though many more developed countries have established protocols that restrict the power of the government over the affairs of an institution, such governance processes are not always understood outside of that country. Thus, when a US, Australian, or British institution, for example, opens an IBC in another country, they are creating a de facto cultural embassy and participating in the affairs of public diplomacy. It has long been recognized that study abroad and other forms of international exchange help to increase intercultural appreciation and may even ease tensions between nonfriendly nation states. However, instead of bringing foreign students to study within a country, nations are now allowing their institutions to set up shop abroad, taking the educational experience to other countries. These institutions provide an opportunity to demonstrate cultural ideals in locations where they may not have been permitted before. Of course, the importing nation is incentivized because the institution can help improve its own educational capacity as well as improve its relative standing in the world.

Conclusion

IBCs have existed for decades, though there has been a recent increase in such entities, as colleges and universities look for new sources of revenues, new ways to enhance their global reputations, and new opportunities to improve the academic experience. Most IBCs are located in developing countries, in environments very different from that of the home campus. As such, individuals responsible for managing and leading IBCs confront a range of challenges that they likely will not have faced elsewhere. This chapter provides an overview of some of the cultural and environmental challenges that IBC leaders will likely confront, discusses three types of boundaries that can impact IBC performance, and lays out issues emerging on the horizon.

Notes

1. Because IBCs as an organizational population are still very young, the exact number of institutions operating at any given time can change quickly as new institutions open and old institutions close.
2. Though non-Western institutions opening in a Western world may face similar obstacles, there seems to be no research on such institutions.

References

Altbach, P. G. 2010. "Why Branch Campuses May Be Unsustainable." *International Higher Education* 58: 2–3.

Becker, R.F.J. 2009. *International Branch Campuses: Markets and Strategies.* London: Observatory on Borderless Higher Education.

Bodycott, P., and A. Walker. 2000. "Teaching Abroad: Lessons Learned about Intercultural Understanding for Teachers in Higher Education." *Teaching in Higher Education* 5 (1): 79–94.

C-BERT. 2011. Branch Campus Listing. Accessed on August 26, 2011, from www.globalhighered.org/branchcampuses.php.

Chambers, G. S., and W. K. Cummings. 1990. *Profitting from Education: Japan-United States International Educational Ventures in the 1980s.* New York: Institute for International Education.

Coleman, D. 2003. "Quality Assurance in Transnational Education." *Journal of Studies in International Education* 7 (4): 354–378.

Debowski, S. 2005. "Across the Divide: Teaching a Transnational MBA in a Second Language." *Higher Education Research and Development* 24 (3): 265–280.

Eckel, P. D., M. Green, and K. Berniaz. In press. "U.S. Providers and Programs Abroad: A Proposed Cross-Border Framework." In *University Futures: Global Markets and the Public Good,* edited by S. Marginson. Dordecht, Netherlands: Sense.

Fegan, J., and M. H. Field. (eds.) 2009. *Education across Borders: Politics, Policy and Legislative Action.* New York: Springer.

Friedman, T. 2005. *The World is Flat: A Brief History of the Twenty-First Century.* New York: Farrar, Strauss, and Giroux.

Hefferman, T., and D. Poole. 2004. "'Catch Me I'm Falling': Key Facts in the Deterioration of Offshore Education Partnerships." *Journal of Higher Education Policy and Management* 26 (1): 75–90.

GLOBAL EXPANSION OF IBCs: MANAGERIAL AND LEADERSHIP CHALLENGES 17

Lane, J. E. 2010a. "Joint Ventures in Cross-Border Higher Education: International Branch Campuses in Malaysia." In *Cross Border Collaborations in Higher Education: Partnerships Beyond the Classroom*, edited by D. W. Chapman and R. Sakamoto, 67–90. New York: Routledge.

Lane, J. E. 2010b. *Higher Education, Free Zones, and Quality Assurance in Dubai.* Policy Paper. Dubai School of Government: Dubai.

Lane, J. E. 2011. "Importing Private Higher Education: International Branch Campuses." *Journal of Comparative Policy Analysis* 13 (4): 367–381.

Lane, J. E., and K. Kinser. 2011. "Reconsidering Privatization in Cross-Border Engagements: The Sometimes Public Nature of Private Activity." *Higher Education Policy* 24: 255–273.

Lane, J. E., and K. Kinser. 2008. "The Private Nature of Cross-Border Higher Education." *International Higher Education* 53: 11.

Levy, D. A. 1986, *Higher Education and the State in Latin America: Private Challenges to Public Dominance.* Chicago: The University of Chicago Press.

Lim, F.C.B. 2008. "Understanding Quality Assurance: A Cross Country Case Study." *Quality Assurance in Education* 16 (2): 126–140.

McBurnie, G. 2002. "Transnational Education, Quality, and the Public Good: Case Studies from South-East Asia." In *Globalization and the Market in Higher Education: Quality, Accreditation, and Qualifications*, edited by S. Uvalic-Trumbic, 159–170. Paris: UNESCO.

McBurnie, G., and C. Ziguras. 2007. *Transnational Education: Issues and Trends in Offshore Higher Education.* New York: Routledge.

Naidoo, V. 2010. "Transnational Higher Education: Why It Happens and Who Benefits? *International Higher Education* 58: 6–7.

Rizvi, F. 2004. "Offshore Australian Higher Education." *International Higher Education* 37: 7–9.

Rostron, M. 2009. "Liberal Arts Education in Qatar: Intercultural Perspectives." *Intercultural Education* 20 (3): 219–229.

Scott, W. R. (2002). *Organizations: Rational, Natural, and Open Systems.* (5th ed.). Upper Saddle River, NJ: Prentice Hall.

Trani, E. P., and R. D. Holsworth. 2010. *The Indispensable University: Higher Education, Economic Development, and the Knowledge Economy.* New York: Rowman & Littlefield.

Verbik, L., and C. Merkley. 2006. *The International Branch Campus—Models and Trends.* London: Observatory on Borderless Higher Education.

Vinen, D. G., and C. Selvarajah. 2008. "A framework for sustainability of an offshore education program: A systems based approach." *Journal of International Business and Economics* 8 (2): 160–169.

JASON E. LANE is an Assistant Professor, Senior Researcher at the Institute for Global Education Policy Studies, and Senior Fellow at the Rockefeller Institute of Government, State University of New York, Albany. He co-leads the Cross-Border Education Research Team (www.globalhighered.org).

Faculty are a critical component to the success of the academic branch campus. In an environment where academic quality is constantly in question, the management and leadership of the academic staff are important, particularly when that staff is spread across multiple geographic locations.

Strategies for Managing and Leading an Academic Staff in Multiple Countries

Rebecca Hughes

Cross-border higher education includes a very diverse set of geographic and managerial relationships. These can range from a "twinning" or a franchise context, where teaching is largely delivered by staff with no academic or contractual relationship directly with each other in different sites, to a "fly-in" situation, where teaching is delivered by a combination of local hires and members of staff from the distant institution who deliver short bursts of teaching, to a full international branch campus model, where the bulk of the teaching is carried out on-site by a range of teaching staff hired for the purpose, often in combination with seconded staff from the distant institution who base themselves at the branch campus for extended periods. The final scenario is the one I experienced and serves as the basis of discussion in this chapter. Whatever the model, the key questions for management will be the same:

- How far can/should you adapt your approach to the local context?
- How do you ensure the quality of teaching and the maintenance of standards across sites?

This chapter begins by describing the broad areas that impact on the task of managing and leading academic staff in multiple countries. In the second half of the chapter, the focus will be on my personal experience with issues that can affect the relationships between "home" and "away" staff and the extent to which these issues can be generalized to other branch campuses.

Fundamentally, the core business of an academic department at a branch site boils down to teaching; research, where applicable; and the

20   MULTINATIONAL COLLEGES AND UNIVERSITIES

administration required to support these two activities. Teaching is the most prominent activity carried out on branch campuses worldwide and is the domain I worked with most closely. In this chapter, the focus is mainly on teaching and the administrative systems to support this.

Background

My experiences in relation to branch campus delivery were primarily gained over a seven-year period setting up and then continuing to support a department delivering English for Academic Purposes (EAP) at a branch campus of the University of Nottingham (United Kingdom) located in Ningbo, China, situated several hours south of Shanghai. A similar department operated at my university's second international campus in Malaysia, but I will be using the China context as my main case study here. The staff and student numbers in the "foundation year programme" rose rapidly in line with a challenging business plan that started with a base of 12 staff and 250 students in 2004. By academic year 2010/11, around 60 internationally recruited EAP teaching staff were delivering programs to approximately 1,400 students annually at the Chinese campus. The bulk of these students are taught on a foundation year that is fully integrated into the following three years of a suite of undergraduate degrees (ranging from English language and literature to engineering). This provides an example of the complexity of combining two regulatory systems. The standard bachelor's degree at the University of Nottingham usually requires a three-year course of study. However, the Chinese higher educational system requires a four-year curriculum; therefore, the foundational year is not optional but regarded as part of the required curriculum at the campus in China.

Considerable effort and time needed to be spent on the processes of recruiting staff with qualifications that matched our UK benchmarks. We decided on a strategy of tight initial control with gradually increased autonomy to deal with the risks involved with, for example, potential staff turnover combined with rapid expansion of student numbers. One of the most challenging aspects of the situation was the changes in management that are perhaps an inevitable consequence of something as dynamic as setting up a campus. During a seven-year period there were four different heads of the EAP team in China and a similarly high level of change in the senior management on site and in the United Kingdom.

A very young organization such as a new branch campus often lacks the implicit knowledge that experienced administration brings. The combination of these factors—change in key staff and rapid growth—meant that there needed to be a "belt and braces" approach to quality management and staffing. Tactics to ensure continuity and stability have included regular two-way visits for key staff, videoconference and extended telephone meetings, clarity over systems of communication and sign-off of materials and assessment information, and encouragement to maintain good housekeeping in terms of records and reporting. The situation has evolved dramatically over the past few years (at both the UK and China campuses) and this dynamism is probably one of the most distinctive features of the relationship.

The management decisions and relationships described here are therefore tailored to a particular context:

- A teaching-led department
- Rapidly expanding targets for student numbers
- Delivery at a full bricks-and-mortar campus
- Teaching embedded in a full degree context across a range of receiving disciplines.

The University of Nottingham has embraced a strategy from an early stage to regard the distant parts of the institution as belonging to a named home department, the head of which would have ultimate responsibility for academic standards. This arrangement influenced the management decisions taken at different phases of the process of establishing the team in China. Nevertheless, the overall situation and challenges will be similar across a range of IBC scenarios, and many of the fundamental issues around leadership cut across these different types of settings.

Identifying the IBC Setting and Expectations of the Teaching Staff

Several factors affect the relationship between the teaching staff at the IBC and the individuals leading those staff from a geographically distant location. First, the relationship is fundamentally influenced by the nature and values of the institution for which the various members of staff work. *University* is a broad term that is applied to educational providers ranging from research-led global players such as Harvard or Yale to niche vocational providers in areas such as information technology.

Even within a geographic region with a considerable amount of shared history, such as that in western Europe, significant differences exist between the roles of faculty and the expectations of what they are required to do. In the United Kingdom, for instance, strong ties exist between research and teaching activities and are generally seen as a defining characteristic of the "Academic." This contrasts with the university systems in continental Europe, where teaching and research tend to be carried out in separate domains (or sometimes in separate institutions). And in the United States, university faculty are generally evaluated on their contributions to teaching, research, and service to the community. It is not uncommon for IBCs to hire staff from these three regions, as well as many others.

The approach to managing teaching staff in an IBC, therefore, is affected by needing to mesh the values of the institution with the expectations of the staff hired from outside the institution. Understanding this is not a straightforward matter. Different institutions, different countries, and different phases in an institution's evolution can influence the role of the faculty. In fact, it is not uncommon for those who work within higher education to constantly reevaluate their professional roles. As Feast and Bretag (2005) noted, tertiary education workers, regardless of their function within the institution, are constantly renegotiating their roles and responsibilities as they try to juggle the competing agendas of the university as a commercial entity and the university as an education provider. At times, it can be even more complicated for the staff of the IBC to situate themselves within the institution as IBCs tend to be relatively young and are simultaneously trying to figure out their role with the larger university organization and the host country environment.

Second, branch campuses differ in the levels of formal and informal integration they promote between the different sites. The type and extent of interaction affects the relationships between the team delivering the teaching and the person responsible for leading them. Integration levels can be seen as the amount of "distance" that the university puts between those delivering the teaching at the branch campus and the parallel set of faculty working at the originating university.

Among IBCs, a variety of interaction patterns can be observed. These range from the aspirations for a fully integrated "portal" system, such as New York University (NYU) in the United States, to a validation agreement, such as the Westminster International University in Tashkent (WIUT), which is an IBC of Westminster University (United Kingdom) located in Uzbek. These are examples at two extremes of a continuum (see also Figure 2.1). In the NYU model, thirteen campuses and educational sites from New York to Singapore and from Abu Dhabi to Paris are seen as equals, allowing staff and students to "flow" between them all. The concept of *home* and *away* is deliberately blurred, and staff and students are encouraged to circulate freely around a number of sites without regarding the geographic location as any barrier to this mobility. In the WIUT situation, a clear distinction is made between the teams and the students on the basis of their location. In this case, there is only a very tenuous connection between the

Figure 2.1. Levels of Staff Integration between Branch Campus and Home Institution

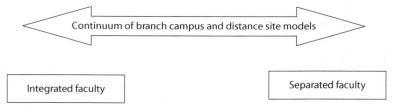

staff delivering similar curriculum at the IBC and those working at the home or validating campus. Clearly, these overarching institutional relationships affect the particular relationships that can exist between leaders and teams.

Whatever the nature of the institution and levels of integration, an IBC is the home of a collection of staff who represent the "brand" of the home institution. Graduates from both locations will have the same degree transcript as a formal record of their time of study bearing the name and the crest of the institution. This "product" of the branch campus will become part of the reputational currency of the named university, with an assumption that the same degree is being recorded and that graduates have the same or closely similar abilities. Negotiations about setting up a branch campus can falter over this issue, as Ben Wildavsky notes in his description of the wooing of Yale to set up an art institute in Abu Dhabi (Wildavsky 2010, 64).

In addition to reflecting academic standards, the teaching staff are often the sole representative of the institution's behaviors and aspirations to the local society and the students being taught. Problems will emerge where the aspirations of the wider institution and the activities at the IBC are not in harmony, or where the institutional philosophy or strategies are not aligned to the needs of the IBC students and the surrounding society. An example of the former would be teaching staff who prefer to teach to the textbook and test facts when the institution is aiming to provide a more autonomous and critical teaching and learning environment for the students. An example of the latter would be a university that fails to provide awards or curricula that meet emerging vocational needs or produces graduates who are unable to gain employment in their own country where particular accreditation is required. (See chapter 1 for additional discussion of some of these cultural and policy disconnects.)

Thought needs to be given to how to instill awareness of what is expected among teaching staff generally, and the reason behind the expectations. Equally, the home university—whatever the degree of integration between sites—needs to become sensitive to what is happening on the ground and listen to what local teaching staff say is needed. Institutional leaders need to understand how they can marry the expectation of providing a comparable educational experience with the restraints and requirements of the distant culture and society. The insights of those involved closely in teaching the students at the IBC are of huge benefit in this process. Nevertheless, tensions can and do arise when the parts of the institution that feel they have much to lose in terms of risk to reputation are asked to consider and/or implement ideas that may only relate to the IBC site. Tricky questions about the identity of learning outcomes, different prioritization of student needs, and differences in teaching and assessment methods can lead to extended (sometimes heated) discussions that need considerable attention.

24   MULTINATIONAL COLLEGES AND UNIVERSITIES

These issues are not confined to the branch campus environment, however, and it may actually be the case that the fresh environment and new staff in the overseas site can provide a clean slate onto which the institution can write an international identity and also set up explicit management and feedback systems that would seem alien in the originating institutional environment. In my own experience, it has been interesting to see how my thinking about these matters has developed over an evolving and long-term relationship with the campus teams, a point I will return to in the conclusion.

The main point to note from the preceding is that it is folly to imagine that delivery to the same standards and outcomes will "just happen." It has to be a process with managerial thought given to it, whatever the management culture of the institution prior to engagement with a branch campus situation. Equally, it is unlikely that putting distance between home and away teams will avoid any reputational effects.

Managing versus Leading versus Administering—Who Does What Where?

The management of teaching staff overseas is challenging and confusion can arise about what is expected from different players in the process. It is helpful to consider the extent of the autonomy that the philosophy of the institution promotes in the different levels or layers of staff. Curricular delivery and approaches can be placed on a four-way matrix (see also Figure 2.2) relating to content and delivery:

- Vertical axis: Fixed content versus evolving content (*what* is required to be taught).
- Horizontal axis: Constrained delivery versus free delivery (*how* the subject is taught).

In a context where there is extremely constrained delivery and a fixed curriculum, the situation will either be a formal franchise or closely resemble a franchise in its nature. There may be specific constraints on the timing and size of classes, for instance, and on the topics to be taught at each stage. Risk is managed by constraining the options of teaching staff and the assumption is that the responsibility for leading any change to the curriculum comes from elsewhere. At the other end of the spectrum is an environment where teaching staff are encouraged to adapt the materials and the curriculum to the local needs of the students and allowed to deliver the material in whatever ways they regard as best. This second type of approach places more accountability on the local team and requires far greater levels of trust and contact between home and away teaching teams. The reason this is an important area to consider is that it has an impact on what is regarded as acceptable in the teaching. In one type of environment abandoning some

Figure 2.2. Four-Way Matrix of Curriculum Development

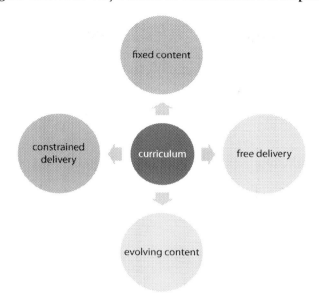

aspect of the curriculum because it is not working might be rewarded, in the other it might lead to a reprimand. There are also implications for those managing the delivery of teaching whether at the IBC or from the home campus. In the context where teaching staff are regarded as professional academic teachers and recruited or professionally developed on this basis there will be greater potential to share responsibilities for quality and teaching resources across the team. Where decisions and changes are solely or mainly in the hands of a higher tier of management, considerable effort is required to maintain the quality of the provision and respond to local need (see Figure 2.3).

Often, the situation is not so clear-cut as this outlining of different models suggests, and in a fast-moving environment decisions need to be made quickly, reacting to an immediate situation. Sometimes this requires home campus staff to make decisions about issues that the IBC staff view as their responsibility. It is important that whenever possible, there should be discussions with IBC managers and teaching staff about the extent of their autonomy so that unnecessary stress is not caused by misunderstandings. A simple flow chart of the quality assurance processes and key dates for suggestions and changes to the curriculum along with who will be the ultimate arbiter can be immensely helpful. This can also become a tool to open up debate and discussion about wider issues of "who does what where" and what the students need currently and in the longer term.

Figure 2.3. Devolved and Less Devolved Scenarios for Quality Assurance

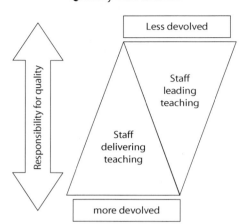

Perspectives of the Individual and Institution

There is often a tension between an individual's career expectations and what his or her institution provides. These issues may be around career progression, salary, terms and conditions (e.g., maternity or sick pay), professional development opportunities, and so on. This is almost inevitable in any employee–employer situation, but the branch campus environment and the nature of university teaching can exacerbate the situation. Some factors that can ease potential problems are:

- **Understand the terms/benefits of employment.** The local manager/head of team or department needs to be well briefed and up to speed on terms and conditions and entitlements—this may require additional support from Human Resources at the home side since these issues can be "make or break" for the individuals concerned. Getting the right information to people when needed is part of the duty of care of the employer at one level and can also become part of the ethos if the institution appears to know and understand how pressing these issues can seem in the branch campus setting. (See chapter 6 for further discussion of some of these issues.)
- **Support professional development.** Relatively small changes and opportunities toward professional development can make a large difference. For example, some IBCs support their faculty and staff to attend professional conferences or professional development seminar series organized through the academic networks of the home institution.
- **Clarify expectations during recruitment.** Make sure that staff are aware of what professional opportunities exist (or not) at the IBC. If there is no

potential for career progression, no right of transfer to another part of the institution, and no realistic opportunity to develop a research career path, then staff in management should not hold out false hopes in this direction.

Beyond dealing with the expectations of the individuals, academic leaders also have to help employees understand and embrace the expectation of the home campus. To this end a more philosophical question to be addressed is whether the outcomes of higher education and the people delivering it can ever be identical in different locations and whether this should be the goal. In terms of a "tight" regulatory approach towards assuring quality, the focus will tend to be on learning outcomes delivered to predetermined criteria rather than a process of localizing knowledge to a different environment. The role of a manager/leader in this relationship is to manage expectations and decide the level of debate about the issues that it is feasible to allow. My sense is that as the branch campus sector matures there will be greater clarity over the contexts in which academic staff are being asked to be careful "deliverers" of prepackaged content (low autonomy, outcomes focused) and contexts in which leadership encourages devolved engagement with the home team to come up with ideas and curricula that are better suited for the environment in which the IBC is located.

Conclusion: Evolving Factors in Leadership and Management

Students are increasingly sophisticated users of the higher education opportunities that are opening up to them as the sector goes global. As McBurnie and Ziguras (2007, 50) note:

> [I]n demand-driven educational provision, what students value about academic work is perhaps more important than what academics value.

If the distance between what students expect from the "brand" of an institution and the teaching and learning experience they receive is too great, they will find a different institution to attend. Faculty are crucial to the experience that the student has, and understanding how to balance the essential characteristics of the institution against changes required by the localization of curriculum is at the heart of the IBC leadership puzzle.

Often, the experience of a faculty member at the IBC is very distant from that of the faculty on the home campus in more ways than geographical setting.

> Too many accounts of teaching in transnational programs begin with an unquestioned view of academic life, in which tenured staff engage in a life's work of research, teaching, and community service within a community of

28 MULTINATIONAL COLLEGES AND UNIVERSITIES

scholars. Invariably, the conditions of work in the branch campus or local partner institution fall far short of this ideal for most commentators, and conclusions generally revolve around the question of how to make academic work in these peripheries more like the traditional ideal (McBurnie and Ziguras, 2007, 50).

This passage highlights the basic questions involved in leading teams charged with providing teaching at an IBC: How similar and how different are the experiences and expectations of staff? What impact do such similarities/differences have on the processes of leading and managing?

Nevertheless, in my opinion, the situation is not simply one of location. As the entire higher education sector matures and faces grand challenges from internationalization and massification, the nature of academic roles taken on by faculty in all but a tiny number of elite institutions will be changed. For example, over the past 30 years, the use of nontenured part-time faculty has doubled in the United States and is increasing in other parts of the world as well (Schibik and Harrington 2004) and the situation described above for the branch campus faculty members may not be that unfamiliar to those delivering teaching on nonbranch campuses.

No one should imagine that in the process of setting up a branch campus an academic ethos can be simply transplanted to a geographically different place. Equally, the process of leading faculty will never be identical, and there is a strong probability that a successful branch campus will have a "washback" effect on the institutional attitudes and behavior of the university that created it. It will be intriguing to see the evolution of the effects of the two-way relationship between the satellite campuses that survive long term and their originating institutions.

References

Feast, V., and T. Bretag. 2005. "Responding to Crises in Transnational Education: New Challenges for Higher Education." *Higher Education Research & Development* 24: 63–78.

McBurnie, G., and C. Ziguras. 2007. *Transnational Education: Issues and Trends in Offshore Higher Education.* London: Routledge.

Schibik, T., and C. Harrington. 2004. "The Outsourcing of Classroom Instruction in Higher Education." *Journal of Higher Education Policy and Management* 26: 393–400.

Wildavsky, B. 2010. *The Great Brain Race: How Global Universities Are Reshaping the World.* Oxfordshire, UK: Princeton University Press.

REBECCA HUGHES is the Pro Vice-Chancellor for Internationalization at the University of Sheffield, United Kingdom. Until March 2011 she was Chair of Applied Linguistics at the University of Nottingham.

3

A common criticism of IBCs is that they cannot recreate the student culture of the home campus. While this is true, some IBCs have gone to great lengths not only to create a comparable culture for their students, but also to integrate their students into the culture of the home campus.

Institutional Ethos: Replicating the Student Experience

Cynthia Howman Wood

International branch campuses (IBCs) have been established in significant numbers over the past ten years (see chapter 1). This phenomenon is particularly pronounced in the Middle East, with a high concentration of IBCs now offering degree programs in countries such as Qatar and the United Arab Emirates. Many observers of this trend have questioned the ability of these institutions both to offer a curriculum and institutional culture that is consistent with what is present at the main campus. While both curriculum and culture are core components of higher education institutions, most administrators, faculty, and policy makers focus on issues of curricular comparability, rarely addressing concerns of shared institutional culture and ethos. Indeed, trying to describe and explain institutional ethos within the context of higher education is a formidable task, as it involves identifying the ideals or foundational beliefs that characterize a community. Yet, as difficult as it is to identify, many college campuses, particularly in the United States, have a very unique campus culture that is an important component of a student's collegiate experience. And it is the shared rituals, stories, and artifacts that help differentiate among educational experiences and helps provide for a shared collegiate experience that often transcends generations of students. Nevertheless, there has been little attention given to how this culture or ethos is transferred from the main campus to an international branch campus. This chapter examines issues of institutional ethos, exploring the multiple approaches taken by Texas A&M University at Qatar (TAMQ) to create an institutional culture similar to that present on the home campus in Texas.

The value of perpetuating a strong institutional ethos cannot be underestimated (Bartell, 2003; Tierney, 1988). Those engaged in professional student affairs practice have long endorsed the notion that a strong institutional

30   MULTINATIONAL COLLEGES AND UNIVERSITIES

culture or ethos encourages and supports student engagement (Kuh, 2009). Students who are fully engaged with their institution are more likely to persist and be academically successful (Pascarella and Terenzini, 2005). According to Kuh and Hall (1993), campus cultures are defined as "the collective, mutually shaping patterns of institutional history, mission, physical settings, norms, traditions, values, practices, beliefs, and assumptions which guide the behavior of individuals and groups in an institution of higher education and which provide frames of reference for interpreting the meanings of events and actions on and off campus" (p. 2). It is a strong campus culture that produces a unique ethos within an institution. Recognizing the need to re-create this ethos at the IBC is essential so that students can benefit from an authentic, comprehensive collegiate experience. A campus without ethos or a unique culture offers little more than an exercise in academic persistence.

When government representatives of foreign countries invite institutions from abroad to establish branch campuses in their countries, the implicit assumption is that they are bringing outstanding academic programming and creating a culturally relevant and socially acceptable campus environment for students that reflects the fundamental ethos that exists on the main campus. Most attention, though, is focused on the development of comparable academic programs; governments and institutions engage in a range of quality assurance practices to ensure such comparability. However, while there is also a corresponding need to develop comparable organizational cultures, the literature is surprisingly silent on how organizational culture is created or re-created at the IBC. One dimension of organizational culture—student culture—will be discussed in this chapter to show how Texas A&M University in Qatar sought to replicate the home campus student experience.

Qatar Education City

The State of Qatar is located in the Arabian Gulf and is a member of the Gulf Cooperation Council (GCC), which includes the United Arab Emirates, Oman, Bahrain, Saudi Arabia, and Kuwait. The Qatar Foundation was established in 1995 by the emir of the State of Qatar, His Highness Sheikh Hamad bin Khalifa al-Thani. Two years later, Education City was created as the postsecondary education branch of the Qatar Foundation to promote world-class higher learning for both Qatari citizens and outstanding students from around the world. Currently, six universities operate branch campuses in Education City: Virginia Commonwealth University, Weill Cornell Medical College, Carnegie Mellon University, Northwestern University, Georgetown University, and Texas A&M University. In addition, there are four other foreign institutions operating in Qatar, but not as part of Education City. These institutions are the University of Calgary at Qatar, the College of the North Atlantic – Qatar, Stenden University, and, most recently, Houston Community College (discussed in chapter 4).

Qatar Education City provides space for the American IBCs to replicate an American style of education, including both the curricular and cocurricular experiences. The Qatar Foundation has constructed a stand-alone building for each campus, and the campuses are encouraged to engage their students in a range of student activities and to help re-create the student experience that exists on the home campus. In each IBC, students are consistently reminded about the connection with the home campus through the use of institutional logos, campus colors, and pictures of the home campus. Some of the IBCs establish exchange programs to allow students leaders on both campuses to visit and learn from each other. Further, it is increasingly common to see students walking around wearing clothing with their university's name and/or logo.

There has also been a long-standing interest by the Qatar Foundation officials to cultivate a common academic and student culture within Education City. When Education City first began, officials wanted the IBCs to have shared general education requirements so that all students would take classes together for their first two years; however, this was not feasible due to the very different degree requirements of each institution. Student culture, however, was facilitated by a student affairs office that works directly for the Qatar Foundation and helps coordinate academic and nonacademic support services for all students. This office is also responsible for running the residence halls and student union, which are shared among all campuses. In addition, the student affairs staff at each campus also work together to create shared experiences such as interinstitutional soccer tournaments and other events. There are competitive collegiate soccer and basketball leagues operating in Qatar largely due to the influence of the Education City universities, particularly TAMQ. Moving forward with the creation of a shared student experience, in 2010 the Qatar Foundation announced the formation of a new entity known provisionally as Education City University (ECU) under the leadership of Sheikh Dr. Abdulla bin Ali al-Thani. The intent of creating the ECU was to optimize the benefits associated with operating six major universities on one campus. In her address to graduates at the May 2010 joint Senior Convocation ceremony at Education City, Her Highness Sheikha Mozah bin Nasser al-Misnad spoke of the Foundation's desire through ECU to focus on the complementary and collaborative activities of the Education City universities "in order to draw maximum benefit from our combined skills and experience."

Development of Texas A&M at Qatar

In 1876, the first public institution of higher learning in Texas began offering classes in College Station. This new institution, originally called the Agricultural and Mechanical College of Texas, was financially supported by funds generated through the Morrill Land Grant Act of 1862, which provided states with funding to support education and research in agricultural

32   MULTINATIONAL COLLEGES AND UNIVERSITIES

and mechanical fields. The name of the institution was officially changed to Texas A&M University in 1963. Students at Texas A&M are commonly referred to as Aggies, a shorthand term for those who attend an "agricultural" college.

Visitors to the main campus of Texas A&M University frequently comment on the distinct nature of the campus. Even for those who have spent time on numerous college campuses across North America and abroad, the intense affinity that most students, staff, and faculty members have to this campus is obvious and pronounced. On any given day, almost all students on the main campus wear an item of clothing or accessory with the Texas A&M University name or logo proudly displayed. When walking through the parking lots, it is difficult to find a vehicle on campus without an A&M decal affixed to the rear window or bumper. The same phenomenon is evident throughout the nearby cities of College Station and Bryan, where most faculty, staff, and students reside. There is an institutional affiliation in this community that is almost cultlike. Whether it is referred to as the spirit of Aggieland or the Aggie Family, it is authentic and highly valued by students, faculty, staff, and friends of Texas A&M University. As the institution's alma mater goes, "But there's a spirit can ne'er be told, it's the Spirit of Aggieland."

The origin and ongoing perpetuation of this ethos is much debated by Aggies and those who try to understand this unique culture. Although there are multiple opinions regarding this topic, there are three recurring themes that are present in most debates about Aggie culture and values: the age of the institution (it is relatively old by US standards), the strong military tradition, and the emphasis placed on collegiate sports (particularly men's American football). When combined, these three factors give rise to a distinct culture that attracts successive generations of families, particularly Texans, to wholeheartedly support the institution.

Texas A&M University at Qatar was established under the auspices of the Qatar Foundation for Education, Science and Community Development in 2003. The responsibility for communicating to students the traditions and values of Texas A&M University typically falls to the department of student affairs. Their efforts are supported by faculty, staff, and members of the institution's leadership team. From the earliest planning stages, there was a desire to develop an authentic Aggie experience in Qatar.

When planning began, there was an immediate awareness that the context of the Qatar campus provided specific challenges given the cultural differences between Texas and Qatar. There was a specific decision that all members of the original student affairs staff should have experience working on the main campus for many years prior to their assuming a role at the campus in Qatar. Their collective knowledge related to Aggie history, traditions, and values was comprehensive and important for helping replicate the Aggie experience. There was a belief that those responsible for re-creating the institutional ethos in Qatar should have firsthand experience living in the culture on the home campus. The collective, intuitive assumption was that as students learn about the history, traditions, and values of the institution, the natural result will be the creation of an institutional ethos grounded in the "Spirit of Aggieland" and also relevant in the Qatari context. The inaugural student affairs staff at TAMQ had to first determine which traditions and values could be presented and perpetuated at the Qatar campus and then design a way to re-create them in the new environment.

Texas A&M Traditions in Qatar

There are several core traditions that are the fundamental building blocks of the Aggie experience and the planning teams leading the development of the Qatar campus were purposeful in identifying traditions that could easily be replicated from the home campus. However, it also became apparent that not all Aggie traditions could be transferred to Qatar. In the following section, the traditions that were easily introduced in Qatar will be discussed first to illustrate the process. In later sections, those traditions that required considerable adaptation will be reviewed as will those that were not considered appropriate for the Qatar campus.

Replicating Traditions. One of the first tasks was to identify a tradition that held great meaning for all members of the Texas A&M community and would be able to engage both students and local alumni living in Qatar. Engaging the local alumni was important both in terms of outreach as well as having additional "experts" to help implement the tradition. Every year on April 21, Aggies around the world gather in over 400 different locations to enjoy an evening of fellowship at the annual Muster. Muster allows current and former students to reconnect and remember those who have passed away during the previous year. On the main campus, current and former students gather at the Camaraderie Barbecue to re-create the experience of the original Muster celebration. Later that evening, the Roll Call of the Absent is read. This roll call honors the memory of current and former students who have passed away since the last Muster. When the names are read aloud, a friend or family member answers "here." A candle is lit to symbolize that those who have passed away are still there in spirit. On the Qatar campus, Muster is attended by large numbers of students, faculty, and staff. Former students from the home campus who are now working in Qatar are also invited to attend. These former students often welcome the opportunity to attend the Muster event hosted at the Qatar campus. Following a dinner, there are several readings by students, a keynote speaker, and then Roll Call is read. Current students stand silently with candles lit to honor Aggies who have passed away the previous year. This tradition has become an important part of campus life in Qatar campus and is an essential link that ties the Aggie experience for students in Qatar to their fellow students in College Station and the former students who reside in Qatar.

34   Multinational Colleges and Universities

Traditions are not only specific events, but can also guide daily interactions. On the home campus there is a specific gesture that many Aggies exchange when they meet. It is a "thumbs-up" sign referred to as "Gig'em." Prior to a football game in 1930, Pinky Downs, a former student (1906) and current member of the Texas A&M Board of regents, coined a phrase of encouragement, "Gig'em Aggies," which is derived from a term used in frog hunting. While exclaiming "Gig'em," the student extended his hand, thumb pointed forward. Today, when Aggies want to encourage their classmates and coworkers, they use this expression and gesture. This practice has been embraced on the Qatar campus, where both students and employees routinely extend their thumbs and enthusiastically say "Gig'em."

The Aggie ring is an important symbolic representation of values and ideals that form the core of an Aggie education. In order to qualify for a ring, undergraduate students must have completed 90 credit hours toward the completion of a degree. Going to the ring office to collect a ring is a special day for all Aggies. In Qatar, the tradition has evolved into a ceremony and celebration held during "Gig'em" week. This event is hosted by the students who form the Traditions Council and supported by the Department of Student Affairs. It is well attended by faculty, staff, and students. On August 29, 2006, the first Aggie ring ceremony was held at the Qatar campus. Students in Qatar are very proud to display their rings as they link them to the larger Aggie family beyond the campus walls. There are several unique logistical issues that had to be overcome in order to continue this tradition in Qatar. The ring is normally made of gold; however, Muslim men are not permitted to wear gold jewelry or adornments. As such, it was necessary to ensure that a ring could be created from other metals. Further, importation of the rings into the country had to be prearranged through the office of Her Highness Sheikha Moza, so that the precious metals could be legally imported into the country.

Two other traditions that help create the local culture focus on athletic teams. Both Maroon Out and the 12th Man have been widely supported on the Qatar campus. The original intention of Maroon Out was to have Texas A&M fans wear maroon colored T-shirts to show support for their Aggie football team. Maroon is one of the school colors. This relatively new tradition started in 1998 when 31,000 Maroon Out T-shirts were sold to Aggies attending the Texas A&M vs. University of Nebraska football game. Now, students at the Qatar campus all receive one Maroon Out T-shirt at the beginning of each academic year. Although students wear these shirts throughout the year, they are most visible on days when the home campus football team plays a game. American football is not played in Qatar; however, both football (soccer) and basketball are very popular sports for male and female students at TAMQ. In addition, a cricket team was sanctioned in 2011 in response to student demand.

All Aggie athletic teams are supported by the "12th Man," which is now a commonly used term to describe the fans of the institution's athletic teams.

New Directions for Higher Education • DOI:10.1002/he

The concept of the 12th Man dates back to a football game played in College Station in 1922. In American football, 11 players are allowed on the field at a time. During the game in 1922, several injuries left only 11 healthy players. Texas A&M football coach, Dana X. Bible, knew that one of the former team members, E. King Gill, was in the stands watching the game. Fearing that he might run out of players, Coach Bible called to Gill and asked him to put on a uniform and join the team in case he might have to play. Gill accepted the call without hesitation. He stood for the remainder of the game, ready to join the team if necessary. Because of his enthusiasm and willingness to support the team, he became known as the 12th Man on the team. Today, all new students are told about the story of the 12th Man and expected to cheer on the university's athletic teams from the sidelines. This tradition is now fostered in the Qatar campus. Whether the team is on the soccer field or the basketball court, the athlete's fellow students are there as the "12th Man" to support the team. Staff and students at the other branch campus institutions frequently comment on the quantity and intensity of the Aggie supporters at sporting events. Over the past several years, the students at the Qatar campus have started to develop their own culturally meaningful adaptations to the 12th Man tradition. Yells (cheers) are chanted in both English and Arabic and traditional Arab drums are brought along to games and played enthusiastically.

Altering Traditions, Preserving Values. In many cases, traditions are embodiments of deeply held values. While some traditions can be replicated easily, there are other examples of how the values can be maintained without duplicating the exact tradition on the home campus. Of course, as discussed later, some shared values seem to emerge with little planning, while others take a great deal more effort. Campus leaders need to understand the cultures of both the home campus and the host country and find ways to appropriately balance both when creating the culture of the branch campus. The following two examples illustrate some challenges to replicating culture and how these challenges resolved.

Texas A&M believes that community service is part of the holistic development of a student. However, few students in Qatar come to the institution with community service experience. In fact, there is little opportunity in Qatar for students to volunteer (it has not been part of that culture) and many students have not previously had to engage in any form of manual labor. In fact, most families in Qatar who are able to send their children to college have domestic help to perform routine tasks at home. To help foster a sense of community engagement, students are encouraged to participate in a local event called Make a Difference Day, which is a collaborative effort of all of the US-based IBCs at Education City. This event is very similar to the Big Event, which is a student-organized day of service on the home campus in which more than 12,500 students, staff, and faculty volunteer their time to help the local community. The goals of both events mirror each other: to encourage students to be active participants in the local

36   MULTINATIONAL COLLEGES AND UNIVERSITIES

community through selfless service to others. During Make a Difference Day in Qatar, students participate in a wide variety of volunteer activities including working with children at the Centre for the Hearing Impaired, pumping gas, cleaning up the campus, and planting trees. It seems now that students at the Qatar campus are widely embracing these activities and participation steadily increases each year.

Another adapted tradition is that of Silver Taps, which is one of the university's most honored traditions. While Make a Difference Day was institutionally planned, the adapted Silver Taps tradition was much more grassroots, emerging from within the student body. The intent of this tradition is to remember and honor current graduate and undergraduate students who have passed away while enrolled. On the first Tuesday evening of each month, a small card with information about each current or former student who has passed away is placed around a specific flagpole on the Texas campus. The lights on the campus are extinguished, students gather around the Lawrence Sullivan Ross statue, and hymns are played on the carillon in Albritton Tower. The Ross Volunteer Firing Squad fires three rifle volleys, and the buglers then play a special rendition of Silver Taps. "Taps is played three times from the dome of the Academic Building: once to the north, south, and west. It is not played to the east because the sun will never rise on that Aggie again" (Texas A&M 2010). There are two sets of barriers that prevent the exact replication of this tradition. First, the tradition is linked to several specific physical locations on the home campus and similar spaces do not exist on the branch campus. Second, the government of Qatar would never allow students at the branch campus to fire weapons in Education City.

However, the death of a Texas A&M student who had spent time on both campuses prompted the creation of an adapted Silver Taps ceremony that could be held in Qatar. In January 2009, Troy Marchang was killed in a car accident. During his time at the Qatar campus, Troy made many friends and was well liked by students and staff. His passing came as a terrible shock to many on the Qatar campus. Upon his death, the students, staff, and faculty at the Qatar campus believed they should honor Troy for his contributions to their campus. Thus, on the same day as the formal Silver Taps ceremony was held on the main campus, a special ceremony was held at the Qatar campus to honor the fallen student. The fact that such a ceremony emerged, after it had been decided not to try to re-create the Silver Taps tradition in Qatar, evidenced the full extent to which the ethos of the home campus had infused the branch campus. Through their participation in the ceremony in Qatar, students and employees demonstrated that they were inextricably linked to the culture and traditions that originated on the main campus.

Respecting Cultural Conflicts. Depending on how different the local cultural is between the home and branch campuses, there are likely to be certain values and traditions that will be difficult or impossible to replicate. It is important for leaders to be conscious of how certain customs on the home campus might violate the mores of the host country or offend the local students.

One example of a tradition that was not able to be replicated is the university's mascot. Most US higher education institutions have mascots, and there is no particular resistance to replicating the idea of mascots at the IBCs. However, the animal that is Texas A&M's official mascot is held in great disregard in the Middle East. The official mascot of the university is a dog. The pure-bred Collie is named Reveille and affectionately referred to as the "first lady of Aggieland." This tradition began in 1931 when a group of cadets accidentally hit a small dog on the way to campus. The dog was brought back to campus so that they could care for her. The next morning when the bugle sounded reveille, the dog started to bark. The dog was thus named Reveille and adopted as the university's official mascot. This is one tradition that will likely never be introduced to the Qatar campus. In many Middle Eastern cultures, including Qatar, dogs are generally seen as unclean and are not welcomed into homes. Many people fear dogs, as they are not regularly exposed to them as are people in the West. There is also the belief that if you have a dog in your home, angels will not enter there. Given the strong cultural disdain for dogs, it would not be appropriate to have one at the Qatar campus, and thus, Reveille has never visited the Qatar campus.

In another example, local mores about the mixing of genders prohibits the use of similar orientation practices on both campuses. Many freshman students in Texas attend a residential camp program designed to orient new students. These coeducational camps are held throughout the summer at an off-campus location and involve a three-day/night commitment. This model of orientation delivery is not an option at the Qatar campus, as mixed-gender overnight activities would be very difficult to deliver, especially for freshman students. Given that most Qatari students have attended single-gender secondary schools, an overnight coeducational orientation would not be supported in the community.

Lessons Learned and Reflections

These traditions help to perpetuate an engaging culture that is shared among students in Texas and Qatar. In addition to what is described earlier, there are several purposeful events and activities each year meant to help educate students about the traditions and culture that exist on the home campus. Orientation activities for new students are robust and include specific information about Aggie traditions and history. Given the relatively small number of freshman students, approximately 125 annually, staff and returning students are able to spend a significant amount of time interacting with students on a one-to-one basis. By learning about the history and traditions associated with the university, students start to develop an institutional affiliation that grows over time. In addition to the orientation activities provided by the institution, the Qatar Foundation Student Life staff delivers an orientation program designed specifically for international students living in residence. This orientation gives freshman students the opportunity to meet peers at the other Education City branch campuses.

To further reinforce the traditions and values supported by the institution, Gig'em Week is held each fall semester. These activities are designed for both new and returning students and college employees. The week starts with a Maroon Out day and Aggieland Market where A&M-branded clothing and accessories imported from the main campus are sold. Other activities include an Honor Code Pledge Signing, Be an Aggie for Life presentation, International Day of Peace service project, Wellness Wednesday, Ring Day celebration, and an Education City Student Leadership workshop. As on the main campus, students in Qatar have formed a Traditions Council. The mission of the council is to preserve and promote the traditions of Texas A&M through education and awareness building. In Qatar, there is a very conscious, proactive effort made to educate students around the traditions, as most students have no prior knowledge of the Aggie experience. This is in stark contrast to many students enrolled at the main campus in College Station, Texas. Many of these students have lived in Texas most of their lives and have significant knowledge about Aggie history and traditions prior to arriving on campus. Students at the Qatar campus have embraced the concept of the Aggie family and are proud to be associated with the university.

Establishing a branch campus in a foreign country is a difficult and complicated task. The complexities associated with planning facilities; designing programs; developing curricula; hiring faculty and staff; establishing an information technology infrastructure; establishing financial systems; developing human resource policies and procedures; working with multiple layers of government; applying admissions standards; recruiting students; establishing relationships with key industry partners; and working in an environment with distinct cultural, religious, and language differences are daunting to say the least. Given the operational focus needed to establish the branch campus, it can be tempting to ignore the need to create an institutional ethos reflective of that which exists on the main campus. A targeted, intentional effort must be made to educate both students and employees about institutional values, history, and tradition. This is particularly important in situations where virtually all students and a significant proportion of faculty and staff have no experience at or knowledge of the main campus. In these cases, students should be encouraged to study at the main campus whenever possible. Opportunities for employees to travel to the main campus and develop positive working relationships with their counterparts should be supported.

The history, values, and traditions associated with Texas A&M University have evolved over the past 134 years. The institution is the heart of the College Station community. Although still in its infancy, the Qatar campus has established a firm foundation upon which the awareness around Aggie history, values, and tradition continues to grow and evolve, with some traditions taking on a uniquely Qatari flavor. The spirit of Aggieland has already become an integral part of the Education City community and is well positioned to become an important part of the larger Qatari community.

References

Bartell, M. 2003. "Internationalization of Universities: A University Culture-Based Framework." *Higher Education* 45: 43–52.

Kuh, G. D. 2009. "Understanding Campus Environments." In *The Handbook of Student Affairs Administration,* (3rd ed.) edited by G. S. McClellan, J. Stringer, and Associates. San Francisco: Jossey-Bass.

Kuh, G. D., and J. E. Hall. 1993. "Using Cultural Perspectives in Student Affairs." In G. D. Kuh (ed.), *Cultural Perspectives in Student Affairs Work.* Lanham, MD: American College Personnel Association.

Pascarella, E. T., and P. T. Terenzini. 2005. *How College Affects Students: A Third Decade of Research.* San Francisco: Jossey-Bass.

Texas A&M University Traditions Council. 2010. In Texas A&M University (database online). College Station, Texas, cited September 12, 2010. Available from http:// traditions.tamu.edu/.

Tierney, W. G. 1988. "Organizational Culture in Higher Education." *Journal of Higher Education* 59 (1): 2–21.

CYNTHIA HOWMAN WOOD is the Assistant Dean for Admissions & Student Affairs at Texas A&M University at Qatar.

This chapter discusses the exporting of the American community college model and the importance of identifying a good "fit" with local partners.

Identifying Fit of Mission and Environment: Applying the American Community College Model Internationally

Mary S. Spangler, Arthur Q. Tyler Jr.

The two-year community college is a hundred-year-old phenomenon, locally funded and distinctly American, yet increasingly exportable. Serving ever more varied roles while being challenged economically, legislatively, and academically to meet progressively higher expectations in the United States, the American community college has been discovered as a valued and essential resource by countries as far-flung as Vietnam and Saudi Arabia, Brazil and Qatar. The focus of most reporting, analysis, and research on international branch campuses (IBCs), however, has been on higher education institutions that export baccalaureate and graduate-level programs to other countries. Community college endeavors on the international stage have received little attention, likely because the institutions themselves are seen as locally based and responsive to community needs, and they have lower-profile stakeholders and students, whose voices carry less impact. The global engagement of community colleges, however, is undergoing rapid and profound change and warrants inclusion in the cross-border higher education literature. Indeed, according to Assistant US Secretary of State Dr. Esther Brimmer (2010), "Interest in community colleges is spreading globally."

As discussed in chapter 7 of this volume, there is an urgent and growing need among developing nations to import foreign educational institutions for the purpose of fostering their own economic development and capacity building. Throughout the world, enrollment in higher education has increased, most of all in developing countries, where professional-oriented programs are those being imported most frequently (e.g., business,

NEW DIRECTIONS FOR HIGHER EDUCATION, no. 155, Fall 2011 © Wiley Periodicals, Inc.
Published online in Wiley Online Library (wileyonlinelibrary.com) • DOI:10.1002/he.443

42   MULTINATIONAL COLLEGES AND UNIVERSITIES

engineering, education) (see, e.g., Kinser et al. 2010; Lane 2010). However, these programs do not provide training in higher-level vocational skill sets often needed to build a robust workforce. As such, many nations and international organizations are exploring ways to provide additional vocational-level education to their citizens in order to build up the core of the world's developing workforce. UNESCO's Education for All campaign is one example of an initiative that is being promoted as a way to import the American community college model. In her speech, Assistant Secretary Brimmer (2010) stated, "Countries are turning to community colleges because they see them as institutions that can serve their local communities." Having a primary purpose to serve local communities in other countries is a rare component of institutions' moving across borders.

This chapter analyzes the benefits, challenges, implementation issues, and key decisions of a community college working outside of its home country. The authors draw upon a case study of Houston Community College (HCC) and its partnerships in Vietnam and in Qatar. The chapter concludes with exportable components, insights, and observations regarding the multinational community college.

Context—The American Community College Model Transported Globally

Most community colleges no longer exist simply in their local communities. External and global agencies impact almost every aspect of the operation, from computers to textbooks, from procurement to tax rates (see chapter 6). If community colleges are to be competitive in the global marketplace, they must not just cope with but excel under these new complex and conflicting conditions. While they began as local institutions, community colleges are not necessarily constrained only to act locally. A tax-supported institution must be able to transcend its physical, place-bound limitations to embrace the world beyond the local community and become an entrepreneurial enterprise. Many within the postsecondary education sector seek to educate their students about being global citizens, able to live and work in the 21st-century environment. Most institutions seek to accomplish this goal by providing local students with the opportunity to engage with international students, participate in internationally focused campus events, or enroll in multicultural classes. That is, they are satisfied to meet what might be called a minimum standard where a foreign language course or an international fair count as evidence of "thinking globally while acting locally." Indeed, that perspective might be characterized as tolerance. However, HCC was not satisfied with what it perceived as mere tolerance. The institution's leadership recognized that global engagements can provide their students with a deeper and more comprehensive international education.

The challenges of workforce development and youth engagement are a critical dilemma facing most nations, and the demand for higher education among young people is growing significantly in emerging nations. The Middle East is one of the regions most in need of opportunities for skill development (Adams 2007). Since the 1990s, there has been a rising divide between the need for skilled, educated workers in the Middle East and North African (MENA) countries and the educational opportunities for the 15- to 25-year-old youth population that has led to a growing dependence on emigrant skilled labor (Aubert and Reiffers 2002). A missing link in most countries is the community college role that facilitates the transition between high school and skilled employment or the university—an institutional mandate to enhance skills of young adults. Community colleges in the United States affect the knowledge and skill development of over 12.4 million people through both credit and non-credit bearing classes, serving approximately 44 percent of all undergraduates in the United States in 2008 (American Association of Community Colleges [AACC], 2010). The interconnectivity of global economic dependency suggests that such knowledge and skill development solutions should be shared among nations. Many nations are, in fact, interested in creating their own community college sector. Few have the capacity or knowledge to do so and are thus looking for assistance from established and successful community colleges in other countries, mainly the United States.

The increasing global interest in community colleges occurred at the same time that HCC was reimagining itself. HCC started with a new vision in 2008, stating that it would be "the most relevant community college in the country." But as noted composer Robert Fritz once pointed out, "It's not what the vision is but what the vision does" (as cited in Senge, Scharmer, Jaworski, and Flowers 2004, 139). HCC leadership used the vision as a stimulus for developing entrepreneurial expansion efforts to create local and global partnerships, taking advantage of the complementarity that existed between local needs and global expansion.

Indeed, it was the local environment that provided a firm foundation for the institution's global engagement. The assets of Houston, Texas, served as the foundational potential to support the institution's new international focus. Houston is the fourth largest city in the United States and has one of the most diverse populations in the United States. Perhaps more important, it is one of the most globally connected economies in the United States, if not the world. Houston's economic pillars include global enterprises in the oil and gas industries, the largest medical center in the world, a transportation multiplex of airports and harbor, NASA, and solid international financial centers (information about the Houston economy and international profile can be found at Houston.org). This total complexity of Houston combined with a growing student population at HCC exceeding 75,000, including more international students than any other community college in the country as according to the *Open Doors* report (IIE Network 2009), and a supportive and diverse economy created the frame against which HCC could reasonably stretch the canvas of this global enterprise.

44   Multinational Colleges and Universities

The manifestation of HCC's engagement was gradual, evolving from participation in international consortia to leading the development of another country's community college sector. The following two examples of limited engagement were leveraged into future opportunities discussed later in the chapter. The first is a niche joint partnership established in June 2008 between leaders from the Brazilian Centro Federal de Educacao Tecnologica (CEFET) system of vocational and technical education—now Instituto Federal do Espirito Santo (IFES) and Instituto Federal Fluminense (IFF)—and five US community colleges. These institutions created a Brazil–US Exchange Network that HCC has maintained, funded originally through a USAID/Higher Education Development grant, to explore common challenges and solutions around issues that shape economic opportunity, prosperity, security, and quality of life in both countries. These activities involve the capacity of community colleges to help create educational initiatives that promote economic development and social mobility by providing and expanding job training opportunities. Partnerships can be formed with local, regional, and federal government agencies, as well as interested private or public agencies. The HCC and IFES/IFF evolved into a pilot project to create an International Center for Education, Language and Technology (ICELT) in Brazil and at HCC for vocational English courses for the oil and gas industry.

A second example is a consulting contract with King Saud University/ Riyadh Community College (RCC) to provide services to secure an independent accreditation for the Saudi institution. Although RCC wanted to emulate the American community college model, the institution also wanted the independence of guiding its own future rather than directly partnering with an American community college. HCC provided support in establishing itself as a consulting entity for accreditation and American community college practices.

Both of these relationships have given HCC the background, experience, and confidence to deliver more ambitious, complex educational services in international settings. Through these endeavors, HCC's leadership discovered that flexibility and the ability to listen to the client's expectations are critical. Potential partners do not automatically want to import the American model in its entirety. Selecting features that respond to cultural, economic, or national needs of the host country may be of higher value than simply replicating an organizational structure, curricular content, or finance model. Expertise and experience in any of these areas on a contractual basis (as was gained from the examples above) build potential for greater opportunities moving forward.

Developing and Leveraging International Partnerships

Opportunities for international partnerships in education abound, but the challenge is to find the right fit for one's institution and the international partner. Community colleges have a defining characteristic within the education system since they have a primary focus on community well-being and development. This is the same motivation that should drive the relationship between the college and its international partner. Thus, there must be more to the partnership than money or prestige. An obvious but often overlooked element is the rationale for the location and nature of the partnership. For example, HCC, because it is located in the oil and gas community of Houston, has a number of advantages to working with other cities where an economic pillar is based on energy. And the large Vietnamese population in Houston helped facilitate connections with Vietnam.

Setting Up a Degree Program in Vietnam. The Houston Community College partnership with the Saigon Institute of Technology leveraged support the college had already been providing the Vietnamese-American community in Houston since 1975. When the fall of the American-backed government of South Vietnam took place, many Vietnamese refugees came to Houston. They found HCC to be a place where they could learn a new trade, acquire English skills, and discover America. Over time, Houston became home to one of the largest Vietnamese-American population in the United States. These immigrants communicated with their family members who remained in Vietnam, including sharing their educational experiences at HCC and the benefits of a two-year community college.

In 1999, discussions began with an educational entrepreneur from Vietnam who had recently obtained permission to open a technical college. He was seeking a US accredited partner. The relationship with HCC developed through discussions with friends and family who resided in Houston and knew of HCC. From this local connection, Saigon Institute of Information Technology entered into a partnership agreement with Houston Community College System in 2000 to provide joint associate of arts degrees in two subjects: computer science technology and business administration. The two-year model of education was a new concept in Vietnam, especially the ideas of merging technical training for workforce certifications and an academic degree from an accredited institution as one way to deliver credibility for students to future employees (Fry 2009). The urgent need of employers for skilled workers and of students for good job opportunities found a positive outcome in the partnership between Saigon Tech in Ho Chi Minh City (formally Saigon) and HCC, whereby Vietnamese students were able to earn HCC degrees without leaving Saigon.

Under the partnership, HCC provides curriculum, credentials, and faculty according to the standards of the Southern Association of Colleges and Schools (SACS), and provides institutional guidance for the management of Saigon Tech. Saigon Tech provides the space and facilities, equipment and supplies, recruitment of students, and general administration as well as teaching nonaccredited courses in various workforce programs.

In 2007, the degree programs were expanded to include joint courses for HCC credit in the associate of applied science (AAS) degrees in accounting,

46   MULTINATIONAL COLLEGES AND UNIVERSITIES

international business, management, and marketing. The primary benefit of this educational relationship is the ability to deliver the community college model of open access to a country emerging into a new technological era so that the development of the workforce can occur in an affordable manner within the boundaries of the country. The Saigon Tech leaders recognized that having a strong program and a quality control process are only two components for success in the labor market. Having students complete a rigorous state-of-the-art program is vital. The partnership between HCC and Saigon Tech enabled almost 1,000 Vietnamese students to earn their AAS degrees from HCC; 250 of these student graduated in 2011.

The final execution of the program encountered several obstacles along the way. The first obstacle was the lingering perception of enmity between the United States and Communist Vietnam created by the tragedies of the Vietnam war. This obstacle could be considered idiosyncratic to the countries involved, although it exemplifies culturally embedded difficulties that could occur anywhere, depending on the specific political or cultural or geographic setting involved in the international relationship. Thus, in this case, initially there were people on both sides who challenged the need for HCC to be engaged in Vietnam, which remains a Communist country. Within Houston, time has allowed much of the local resistance fostered from the Vietnam war to fade, and the new political sensibilities to the global economy helped many recognize in global education partnerships the means to create understanding and trust. What was originally perceived as a barrier by some now may be seen as a success. The Vietnamese Consul General in Houston recently hosted a celebration of 15 years of normalized relations between the two countries. Houston Community College and Saigon Tech's partnership is among the pillars that he proclaimed has aided in cementing this transformation and lasting relationship.

The second obstacle was a belief that needs of communities around the home campus are the only interest that community colleges should serve. There were often many questions about why a community college, which was funded locally, should be serving other communities, particularly those outside of the country. It was important to explain, as discussed earlier, that both HCC and the general Houston area benefit from such global engagements. In fact, the types of engagements pursued by HCC were directly linked to the environmental conditions that existed within Houston.

A final obstacle was political and cultural differences that existed between Houston and Vietnam (an issue discussed throughout this volume). As is the case for many transnational educational operations, culture can have a significant impact on teaching and learning, particularly when the educational systems are based on different pedagogical approaches (Bodycott and Walker 2000; Rostron 2009) such as is the case between the United States and Vietnam. One particular challenge is in meeting accreditation requirements (see chapter 5 for additional detail on US quality assurance procedures). Everything done at Saigon Tech leading to an HCC degree must meet the same standards as if the courses and students were in Houston. In addition to ensuring the curricular comparability, there is also a challenge in finding qualified staff. The faculty, who are primarily Vietnamese, must have academic preparation from institutions of higher education recognized by US accrediting agencies and must be credentialed as if they were teaching at HCC in the United States. The cultural differences are compounded by the existence of two distinct government structures: communist and democratic. These differences can manifest themselves in the governance of the local campus and create tensions between the staffs of HCC and Saigon Tech (see also chapter 2). Given the differences in culture and distance between Texas and Vietnam, maintaining these standards requires diligence, respect, communication, and trust, based on two different value systems.

The Qatar Experience. The connections between Houston and Qatar were even more widespread and made development of a partnership between the two easier than it might seem at first glance. Houston is a world center for oil and gas production and has additional economic pillars in health, transportation, and finance. Its long-standing association with the oil and gas industry creates an economic and cultural commonality with the nation and the people of Qatar. Likewise, Qatar's capital, Doha, is a market leader in the oil and gas industry in the Middle East, is establishing a new pillar of economic development in the medical and finance arenas, and has an expatriate population that is composed of individuals from more than 120 countries. Qatar has developed a five-star airline with the only nonstop access to Doha from Houston. One of the primary Texas Medical Center partners, Methodist Hospital, has started the development of a new hospital in Doha. The Qatari consulates in the United States are located in Houston and New York City. The country has recently started the development of its third liquid gas terminal just outside Houston. This multibillion-dollar project will create hundreds of new jobs in the community and surrounding area. All of these connections made HCC a good fit for helping Qatar develop its community college system. Moreover, Houston's ethnic and cultural diversity makes it generally accepting of others and new ideas.

The events and circumstances that led to the development of a relationship with Qatar were completely different from those surrounding Saigon Tech. Unlike the private-public partnership with Saigon Tech, where an entrepreneur selected HCC, the partnership with Qatar is a public-public one, won through a stiff competitive process. In fact, Qatar has been increasingly turning to foreign education providers to help build local capacity and serve the Qatari community (Lane and Kinser 2011). Qatar had invested in a university system, which promulgated Qatar University in 1973 and more recently partnered through the Qatar Foundation with six US universities when it initiated major educational and cultural expansion beginning in 1995 with the creation of the Qatar Foundation and Education City. This is in addition to branches of a Canadian university, a Canadian

48   MULTINATIONAL COLLEGES AND UNIVERSITIES

community college, and a Dutch university that operate independently in Doha. However, Qatar had decided that none of these offer the level of accredited skill development or academic access needed for all Qataris to be successful in skilled employment or transfer to accredited universities. Studies showed a great need to fill an access gap in Qatar educational opportunity (Stasz, Eide, and Martorell 2007). Qatar wanted a second tier of higher education that would feed its workforce and offer an additional pathway into the baccalaureate-granting institutions. The Qatari leadership, as part of their strategy for national success and educational reform, recognized that their people needed at least 14 years of knowledge and skill development in the new global economy and so decided to create the Community College of Qatar (CCQ). In order to create an institution that would be able to provide "for university transfer coursework and career coursework focused on the Qatar workforce needs, . . . a select group of academic and industry representatives put in place an extensive and comprehensive process to choose the CCQ's partner college," according to the chairman of the CCQ Steering Committee (April 20, 2010). Led by Her Highness, Sheikha Mozah bint Nasser Al Missned, the Qatar government started the process to develop a community college. The identified gap in access to Qatar higher education and learning for personal, workforce, and national development drove the decision to select the CCQ partner college.

The first decision made after review of the various types of community and two-year colleges worldwide was to create a system based on the US model of community colleges. The Qatari Supreme Education Council (SEC) developed a subcommittee, headed by the former president of Qatar University. Initially, seven colleges and a consortium were invited to submit a partnership proposal. Finalists were also asked to defend their proposal via videoconference. Elements of the actual proposal included scope of services, timeline, staffing, organizational chart, job descriptions, price structure, and curriculum options. These interactions, along with the visit of at least two of the teams in Doha and proven success in international initiatives, were vital to the SEC's selecting HCC. In this partnership, HCC has established Qatar's first community college.

Unlike Saigon Tech, the creation of a turnkey system in Doha required the selection and credentialing of 43 HCC staff who had to relocate in Doha. All of these HCC employees have been seconded to work for the Community College of Qatar and aid in its development. The goal is to serve Qataris with educational services, support, and academic knowledge and adapt the American model ultimately to their culture. The initial class of 304 students started their studies on September 26, 2010. Over the next five years, this small cohort of students is expected to grow to an annual enrollment of 2,000 students in several locations in Doha and eventually to other Qatari communities. Likewise, the number of HCC seconded employees will grow to about 100. Ultimately, the SEC intends to end its partnership with HCC and secure independent regional accreditation from the United States for

CCQ and offer its own courses and programs and hire its own faculty and administration.

Some of the added challenges to overcome in the process of opening a college in support of a sovereign nation with seconded employees included identifying people who could adapt to a foreign culture and live in a place with different norms. Establishing a campus is challenging even within the United States, but building one on the other side of the world requires experience, organization, and strategic planning skills at the mastery level. Everything from furniture to textbooks, from assessing to orienting students, from developing a class schedule to creating an academic calendar is done with seconded staff in Qatar and administrators based in Houston coordinating and advising by teleconference, Internet, and periodic travel (see also chapter 2 for information about coordinating staff from afar). Housing, school for dependent children, transportation, health care for employees and dependents, and socialization are just a few of the critical items that must be addressed to ensure that faculty and staff are comfortable in their new setting so they can focus on the mission of teaching and learning for students. These issues are further exacerbated by the time and workweek differences. Like most American institutions, HCC's workweek goes from Monday through Friday, while CCQ operates from Sunday through Thursday (a norm in many Middle Eastern countries). Given the nine-hour time difference between Houston and Doha, there are only six hours each week that the two administrations and faculty teams can easily interact. Also challenging was changing the modality of how faculty interact with students, who in Houston are primarily part-time. Unlike in Houston, students in Doha are full-time and have a different set of expectations than their US counterparts. All these challenges require patience and determination if success is to be realized.

Exportable Components

The American model of education is flexible in being able to meet the needs of both the individual and the employer, across the academic lifespan of the student. There will likely be increased interest for the American model of community college education for millions of people around the globe (personal communication, October 20, 2010, Dr. Esther Brimmer, Assistant Secretary of State, Bureau of International Organization Affairs, ACCT 41st Annual Leadership Congress, Toronto, Canada). Indeed, over half of all international branch campuses around the globe are from the United States (Becker 2009; C-BERT 2010). As an educational institution, HCC has provided the leadership in transporting the American community college model abroad and provided the credibility by demonstrating the potential for its growth and enrichment to Vietnam and Qatar.

The following are the key components that make the American community college a successful exportable model for emerging and developing countries:

50 MULTINATIONAL COLLEGES AND UNIVERSITIES

- Community colleges focus on learning and teaching and can deliver an educated workforce affordably, efficiently, quickly, flexibly, and responsively, especially in countries where trained, skilled workers are increasingly in demand. They design and deliver instructional packages in a wide variety of workforce programs.
- Community college administrators are experienced in working closely with local communities and in partnership with small businesses and corporate entities to design curriculum to respond to the needs of the region or country and deliver the training and knowledge that will have a positive impact on economic development.
- Community college administrators have the expertise to adapt the community college model to individual countries and to support curriculum development, revision, and expansion to respond to the needs of the local communities through designing customized training for the country and/or the business whether it be a modular, online, or on-site format.
- Community college management and faculty can provide technical assistance and expertise to emerging postsecondary institutions seeking their own accreditation.

Insights and Observations

The decision to expand Houston Community College's reach internationally has not been a simple one, nor was it easily or quickly made. It has met with resistance among those who fear the loss of local resources beyond their borders or loss of their control, who worry about the drain of talent to other locations without seeing the upsides of investments that bring the possibility for greater return, who focus on the confusion of institutional mission and vision instead of the opportunity for enrichment of resources, and who want to wall out the unfamiliar or unfriendly cultures in lieu of including the richness of diversity. But the value of the American community college model makes the expansion the right thing to do. This value-added initiative positioned HCC, already considered the leading internationalized community college in the country, to be at the forefront of international initiatives.

Unequivocally, one of the most important areas to address is that there be no associated cost to local taxpayers and no negative impact on HCC's operating budget. Thus, the college is not the consumer of services but the expert or consultant whose services are sought. Moreover, administrative time must be minimally impacted, although with today's ubiquitous and sophisticated technology most competent and efficient administrators are expected to be in constant daily contact regarding activities.

The intent is not to ignore local needs, but rather to develop a range of international engagements and leverage them to serve students and communities in the home country. HCC can now provide students who want to learn and/or work outside the United States a chance for exposure to the global economy. Such experience can open doors with multinational employers through job opportunities in international business. Summer programs, faculty exchanges during the academic year, and a pathway for financially needy Texas students and those from underrepresented groups to participate in a study-abroad learning experience are now part of the long-term trajectory of HCC. And when a cohort of faculty is dispatched to another country for an extended period to work as "a community of interest," the opportunity to impact the home campus is a reality on their return.

The American community college model can be used to help international relationships, strengthen domestic economic development, support national security, and create hope across the populations in the international arena. This enterprise could provide the missing link for emerging and developing nations to transform themselves and optimize valuable resources—their human capital.

References

AACC. 2010. American Association of Community Colleges—Fast Facts. Retrieved July 2, 2011, from www.aacc.nche.edu/AboutCC/Pages/fastfacts.aspx.

Adams, A. V. 2007, February. *The Role of Youth Skills Development in the Transition to Work: A Global Review.* Washington, DC: World Bank.

Aubert, J., and J. Reiffers. 2002. *Knowledge Economies in the Middle East and North Africa: Toward New Development Strategies.* Washington, DC: World Bank.

Becker, R. 2009, October 20. *International Branch Campuses: Markets and Strategies.* London: Observatory for Borderless Higher Education.

Bodycott, P., and Walker, A. (2000). "Teaching Abroad: Lessons Learned About Intercultural Understanding for Teachers in Higher Education." *Teaching in Higher Education* 5 (1): 79–95.

Brimmer, E. October, 2010. "Keynote Speech: Association of Community College Trustees Congress." Toronto, Canada.

C-BERT. 2010. List of international branch campus. Retrieved on February 15, 2011 from www.globlahighered.org.

Fry, G. W. 2009. "Higher Education in Vietnam." In *The Political Economy of Educational Reforms and Capacity Development in Southeast Asia,* edited by Y. Hirosato and Y. Kitamura, 237–261. New York: Springer.

IIE Network. 2009. "Open Doors 2009 Report on International Educational Exchange, Community College Data Resource, Top 40 Associate's Institutions Hosting International Students, 2008/09." Retrieved October 30, 2010, from http://opendoors.iienetwork.org/page/155892/.

Kinser, K., D. C. Levy, J. C. Silas Casillas, A. Bernasconi, S. Slantcheva-Durst, W. Otieno, et al. 2010. "The Global Growth of Private Higher Education." *ASHE Higher Education Report* 36(3). San Francisco: Jossey-Bass.

Lane, J. E. 2010. *Higher Education, Free Zones, and Quality Assurance in Dubai.* Policy Paper. Dubai: Dubai School of Government.

Lane, J. E., and K. Kinser (2011). "Reconsidering Privatization in Cross-Border Engagements: The Sometimes Public Nature of Private Activity." *Higher Education Policy* 24: 255–273.

Rostron, M. 2009. "Liberal Arts Education in Qatar: Intercultural Perspectives." *Intercultural Education* 20 (3): 219–229.

52 MULTINATIONAL COLLEGES AND UNIVERSITIES

Senge, P. M., C. O. Scharmer, J. Jaworski, and B. S. Flowers. 2004. *Presence.* New York: Doubleday.

Stasz, C., E. R. Eide, and F. Martorell. 2007. *Post-secondary Education in Qatar: Employer Demand, Student Choice, and Options for Policy.* Doha: Rand-Qatar Policy Institute.

MARY S. SPANGLER *is chancellor of Houston Community College, the fourth largest community college in the United States with approximately 75,000 students each semester.*

ARTHUR Q. TYLER JR. *is deputy vice chancellor and chief operating officer of Houston Community College.*

This chapter highlights the dilemmas facing traditional models of quality assurance in a global environment where higher education institutions can and do cross geopolitical borders.

Multinational Quality Assurance

Kevin Kinser

Multinational colleges and universities pose numerous challenges to the traditional models of quality assurance that are designed to validate domestic higher education. When institutions cross international borders, at least two quality assurance protocols are involved. To guard against fraud and abuse, quality assurance in the host country is concerned with authorizing education offered only by reputable foreign institutions and determining whether the branch can fulfill its educational obligations to local students. Quality assurance procedures that apply to the home campus, however, must verify that the institution continues to fulfill its educational obligations domestically, while guarding against reputational or financial concerns raised by any off-campus programs.

There is, therefore, an inherent tension between the quality assurance procedures at home and those in place within the host country. Each side must guard against improper or inferior practices arising from competing expectations for the branch campus mission. Compounding the difficulty is the fact that there are few quality assurance structures in place that can easily cross international boundaries (Kinser 2009; Uvalić-Trumbić 2007). Indeed, there are currently no recognized multinational quality assurance regimes that can serve as a trusted gatekeeper on a global scale, and regional efforts at standardizing national quality assurance efforts are in their infancy.

The purpose of this chapter is to provide an overview of multinational quality assurance to help leaders of IBCs and their home campus colleagues understand the unique quality issues that emerge when a college or university crosses international borders. The first section discusses the concept of quality assurance, including how quality emerged as a significant issue for higher education over the past quarter century. The chapter then focuses on the range of external quality assurance processes in existence, using brief case descriptions from several countries to highlight the major strategies

54   MULTINATIONAL COLLEGES AND UNIVERSITIES

employed by both importing and exporting countries. The emerging field of multinational quality assurance will be discussed in the third section, highlighting various attempts at standardizing and integrating national and regional models.

What Is Quality Assurance?

Quality assurance is a relatively new concept in higher education. Even though systems of quality assurance can be traced back more than a century in the United States and the United Kingdom, few other countries developed their own systems before the mid-1980s. What started then as a trickle of reforms and new systems in a handful of countries became a tsunami in the 1990s. An international association for quality assurance agencies was founded in 1991 with eleven charter members representing nearly all of the countries with formal quality assurance regimes at the time. By 2007, that association had 154 members from seventy-eight countries (Lewis 2009). In less than twenty years, quality assurance has become a global phenomenon.

The multifaceted diversification of many higher education systems and the growth of private sector institutions explain the emergence of quality assurance policies during the 1980s and 1990s (Sanyal and Martin 2007; Uvalić-Trumbić 2007). When the government is the exclusive provider of a service, legitimacy flows directly from the authority of the nation. There are no accrediting agencies for post offices, for example, and external quality assurance does not exist for state highway departments. In the same way, old government-dominated systems of higher education, *ipso facto*, found little urgency in proving their own worth. The development of private-sector institutions, exploding student demand, and a coincident erosion of trust in public entities, however, created urgency, first for the evaluation of new educational entities, then emerging, and eventually for all higher education institutions.

The use of the term *quality assurance* has changed over time to reflect society's growing interest in evaluating the performance of institutions of higher education (Sanyal and Martin 2007). Current use suggests a comprehensive term that refers to all of the policies, procedures, and activities that are used to validate and improve the performance of a higher education institution (Harvey 2011). Within this definition, quality assurance is usually subdivided into internal and external processes. Internal quality assurance follows the historical view that colleges and universities are intrinsically motivated by the noble pursuit of truth. As such, they should be trusted to identify and correct substandard activities or outcomes on their own accord. External quality assurance, however, reflects the post-1980s view that quality must be validated by stakeholders outside the institution, typically through quality audits or assessments or an accreditation process. External quality assurance is not necessarily government controlled, though it tends to be established in response to public policy demands—in particular, the need for greater accountability (Harvey 2005; Lewis 2009).

Finally, quality assurance presumes that one knows what quality in higher education actually is (van Ginkel and Dias 2007). Three definitions for quality are generally cited in the literature: fitness for purpose, or how well it fulfills its objectives; fitness of purpose, or the relevance of higher education to societal needs; and standards-based, or whether it meets stated criteria for performance (Sanyal and Martin 2007). In addition, most statements equate quality in higher education with serving the public good (e.g., UNESCO 2005). This means that quality in higher education is not typically measured by bottom-line efficiencies, but rather is distinguished by connecting institutional mission to outcomes valued by both the institution and external stakeholders (Kinser and Hill in press).

External Quality Assurance for Multinational Colleges and Universities

External quality assurance has always been designed to operate on the national level. Serving the public good refers to the domestic public good, and the primary target for quality assurance has been institutions operating only in the home country. With the expansion of cross-border higher education, however, external quality assurance developed to consider both the import and export of academic programs and institutions. Still, though, the focus is explicitly national. For exporting nations, external quality assurance seeks to protect the domestic institution from reputational, academic, or financial damages caused by inappropriate activity outside the country (McBurnie and Zyguris 2007). For importing countries, the quality assurance regime is designed to guard against low standards, financial impropriety, or competition detrimental to the domestic system of higher education.

Some importing countries discourage foreign higher education by putting into place entry barriers, partnership requirements, and majority ownership restrictions. Although these may be seen as regulatory issues separate from assessing and discriminating among IBCs based on quality, they tend to be included as part of the country's quality assurance regime and are often justified by quality claims (Cheung 2006).

Exporting Countries. The following section briefly summarizes the quality assurance procedures associated with the establishment of IBCs in selected countries. The leading exporting countries are the United States, United Kingdom, and Australia.

United States. The United States operates a voluntary, nongovernmental accreditation model for external quality assurance. Institutions are typically under no obligation to participate in external quality assurance, and the government role is formally limited at both the federal and state levels. In practice, though, nearly all legitimate institutions of higher education are accredited, and the federal government has assumed an important function by linking eligibility for financial aid to approval by a recognized accreditation agency. Still, as a nongovernmental function, there is no such thing as

56   MULTINATIONAL COLLEGES AND UNIVERSITIES

accreditation by the US government or any particular state. Confusion on this point has been exploited by unaccredited for-profit institutions seeking to establish relationships abroad (Kinser 2010).

There are dozens of accreditation agencies in the United States, though nearly all of the identified IBCs from the United States are accredited by one of six regional accreditation agencies. Standards vary somewhat between agencies, but all follow a similar peer review process that results in a dichotomous decision regarding whether or not the institution as a whole, including the branch campus, meets minimum stated criteria. As a consequence, a low-quality IBC may put the accreditation of the home campus itself at risk. Evaluative reports of the accreditation agency, however, are not made public. Typically, only whether or not the institution has been accredited is revealed by the agency.

Regional agencies in the United States have endorsed a common set of principles related to the review of overseas programs (Principles of Good Practice in Overseas International Education Programs for Non-U.S. Nationals 1997). These principles specify that the home institution is responsible for anything done in its name, regardless of the ownership model of the branch or any partnership arrangements in place, and prohibits the franchising or selling of its name. They stipulate that standards for IBC programs are equivalent to those of the home campus, and that they meet US accreditation agency standards. Program equivalency is maintained by requiring any credits awarded at the overseas branch to be applicable to degree programs at the home campus. The programs, however, may be adapted to the culture of the host country. Admission standards must be similar on each campus, and all students are recognized as students of the US institution. An administrator employed by the US institution must be resident at the IBC to provide direct oversight of the educational quality of the foreign program. Other principles address mission compatibility, public disclosure requirements, and contractual arrangements.

United Kingdom. Even though the UK external examiner program goes back over one hundred years, the current system of external quality assurance evolved coincident with the 1980s, and 1990s, period of global quality assurance emergence (Universities UK 2008). The system retained the use of externally evaluated exams administered to students at the end of each term and established multiple bodies to review different levels of education and assess the quality of teaching and learning for each subject. In 1997, these external reviews of teaching and learning began to be taken over by the newly formed Quality Assurance Agency for Higher Education (QAA). This body reviews how all higher education institutions in the United Kingdom maintain quality, evaluates their processes, and reports its findings to the public and government funding bodies. In the United Kingdom, all colleges and universities are legally autonomous degree-granting institutions that award academic credentials by their own authority. Thus, the QAA can only publicize poor quality institutions and in itself cannot take away the authority to operate, though funding decisions by the government are informed by the results of the QAA evaluation. There are a few differences among the procedures in England, Northern Ireland, Scotland, and Wales, but none that are directly relevant to multinational colleges and universities.

The main guidance concerning quality assurance for IBCs comes from Section 2 of the *Code of Practice for the Assurance of Academic Quality and Standards in Higher Education* (Quality Assurance Agency [QAA] 2010). Section 2 contains "precepts" for maintaining quality in programs offered in collaboration with other entities and specifically includes IBC activity under its purview. The precepts specify that the home campus is responsible for all academic awards granted under its authority, and that all awards should meet the expectations of the full *Code of Practice*. The home campus must retain sole authority to award credentials. Financial arrangements should be designed to avoid "temptations" that could compromise quality. The home campus must retain final responsibility for the appointment of external examiners; their training and performance should be consistent with normal home campus practices.

Most of the precepts, however, are directed toward defining and delimiting the relationship of the home campus with a partner organization. These state that the name and location of any partner must be listed on the certificate and/or transcript, and insist the institution conduct due diligence on any potential partner. Partners are also expected to hew to the guidelines expressed in the *Code of Practice*. "Serial" programs, where the partner organization passes on academic programs or functions to a third party, are discouraged but not prohibited. Other precepts detail the need for written contracts and that programs are accurately and fully described to potential students.

In addition to the institutional audit, QAA review of IBCs occurs on a country-by-country basis (Jackson 2006). A single country is selected, and all international activities by UK institutions in that country are reviewed. Audits follow similar principles and processes as the institutional audit, but they do not occur at the same time or on the same schedule. To date, overseas audits have occurred in Malaysia, Greece and Cyprus, India, China, and Hong Kong (QAA 2011).

Australia. External quality assurance at the federal level in Australia is a rather recent phenomenon, only emerging in 2000 with the creation of the Australian Universities Quality Agency (AUQA). AUQA was established by commonwealth, state, and territory ministers for higher education as a nonprofit organization that operates independently of higher education institutions. It is funded primarily by the ministers, though it maintains an independent board of trustees. AUQA is charged with conducting quality audits of all Australian higher education institutions and accreditation

58   Multinational Colleges and Universities

authorities, and making public reports of institutional performance and outcomes. All universities in Australia are self-accrediting, and each state or territory has procedures for accrediting nonuniversity institutions. Thus, AUQA conducts external quality assurance for all universities and nonuniversities, as well as the government bodies responsible for accrediting nonuniversity entities.

The scope of AUQA audits includes all the academic activities carried out in the Australian institution's name, and the agency has devoted substantial attention to "transnational arrangements" (AUQA, 2008). Site visits to the home campus are standard. Procedures for evaluating overseas activities of Australian campuses have a separate policy. Revised in 2004, overseas audit procedure adopts a risk assessment approach to determine whether the institution's activities abroad warrant a physical inspection. Seven factors are considered, including the size and scope of the activity, its significance to the institution, potential for problems with the activity, the applicability of host-country quality assurance mechanisms, and the practicality and necessity of conducting a site visit (Woodhouse, 2006). Site visits typically will involve no more than two AUQA auditors visiting one or two foreign locations. Rarely will AUQA decide that no overseas visits are necessary. A separate report of the site visit is not made public, but is used to inform the home campus audit and final public report (Kristoffersen, 2006).

The audit is guided by a 17-point framework that requires AUQA to consider a range of issues related to the relationship between the home campus and its overseas programs. AUQA does not presume that the institution will offer the same programs abroad as it does at home—programs can be "identical, equivalent, significantly tailored or unique"—but all programs must be specifically approved for the foreign campus. Attention is given to the host-country quality assurance procedures and relationships with the local community. Cultural issues are also evident in the review, with both program characteristics and faculty training expected to be modified with respect for local context. Other points suggest the need to consider the extent to which research functions are supported as part of the overseas activities, due diligence in selecting partners, and developing clear contractual and governance relationships.

A new entity is being formed in Australia, the Tertiary Education Quality and Standards Agency (TEQSA). Beginning in 2012, TEQSA will take over the responsibility for quality assurance and regulation now currently shared by AUQA and government authorities.

Importing Countries. The following section reviews the quality assurance procedures in two of the leading importers of IBCs.

Dubai. IBCs represent the majority of higher education institutions in Dubai (Kinser et al. 2010), and the emirate represents an environment that is still working through its regulation of IBCs. The state and federal governments have yet to fully agree upon how IBCs are to be regulated, as there is a lack of clarity over who is responsible for the institutions (Lane 2010). Under current policies, all IBCs in Dubai must receive an Educational Services Permit from Dubai's Knowledge and Human Development Authority (KHDA). KHDA requires every program offered to be accredited, and permits must be renewed annually. External quality assurance is therefore mandatory in Dubai, as no IBC can be established or continue to operate without the validation required by the KHDA permit.

IBCs may choose to have their programs accredited by either the federal accreditation body for the United Arab Emirates, which evaluates them along the same standards as all domestic campuses, or have their programs validated by the University Quality Assurance International Board (UQAIB) in Dubai, which recognizes that IBCs are extensions of an educational institution in another country. UQAIB members are international experts on quality assurance from Australia, Denmark, Hong Kong, India, New Zealand, Saudi Arabia, the United Kingdom, and the United States. They do not represent UAE institutions or ministry officials. Approval requires that the IBC demonstrate that its institutional policies and procedures are substantially equivalent to the home campus. The IBC must also meet requirements from a reputable external quality assurance agency, typically an agency from its home country. UQAIB does not typically conduct site visits, but rather reviews submitted documentation from the branch to confirm that all programs and activities are equivalent to those at the home campus. In particular, UQAIB verifies that any program offered at the IBC is also offered on the home campus. UQAIB approval can be for up to five years.

The process is designed to accommodate a wide variety of institutional activity without making standardized judgments on quality separate from what the home campus and quality assurance procedures dictate (Rawazik & Carroll, 2009). As a new process, the viability of the model has not been tested, though it has resulted in the closure of at least two campuses for failing to meet UQAIB standards.

Malaysia. External quality assurance emerged in Malaysia in response to the growth of private-sector institutions during the 1990s. Separate quality assurance systems were maintained for public and private institutions, and, in a simple form of quality control, degree-granting authority was initially limited to only those private institutions that developed partnerships with foreign campuses. Later, private institutions were given permission to offer their own degrees, and IBCs were also welcomed as part of the degree-granting private sector. In 2007, the Malaysian Qualifications Agency (MQA) was established to unify the higher education system in Malaysia. It was tasked with implementing a qualifications framework that would define standards and accredit all tertiary institutions and academic program levels. The MQA is an agency of the Ministry of Higher Education, but participation in a program or accreditation review is voluntary for all institutions, domestic or foreign. Benefits of accreditation, however, include credit transfer, ability for students to participate in student loan programs, and eligibility for civil

60   Multinational Colleges and Universities

service employment. Consequently, almost all institutions have undergone review, including four IBCs.

The MQA quality assurance procedures make few distinctions between public or private institutions, and do not discriminate based on foreign status. IBCs are treated as private-sector institutions in terms of ministry classifications, which means they have more flexibility in some admission requirements and language of instruction than do their public-sector peers. But all quality assurance procedures are the same for all institutions under the new framework, guided by an institutional audit based on the Code of Practice for Institutional Audit last revised in 2009. The Code includes nine areas for evaluation, none of which specifically address IBC activities other than noting that any academic and/or financial partners must share the responsibility for program monitoring and review. A summary of the audit report is made available to the public.

After initial accreditation is granted, further audits may be used to determine whether institutions should become self-accredited. In other words, they would be able to accredit their own programs going forward without applying to the MQA. The IBCs operating in Malaysia that had graduated students were selected for this review, along with four public-sector research universities. All eight institutions were approved as self-accredited institutions.

Multinational Quality Assurance

The nationally based models for quality assurance pose challenges for multinational colleges and universities that must concurrently work with different quality assurance processes in multiple countries. Conflicts can occur when the policies in the host country conflict with those of the home country. For example, the Dubai requirement that institutions only offer programs at the branch that are also offered on the home campus is not necessarily supported in Australia with an AUQA audit that allows IBCs to substantially deviate from home campus practices. Moreover, acceptable practice varies depending on the quality assurance regime, such as the prohibition on franchising in the US case and the acceptance of it by the UK QAA.

Several efforts have been made to develop a transnational quality assurance regime, but few have directly contemplated abolishing national models. More often, proposals have sought the cross-border recognition of quality assurance procedures through the global or regional adoption of a set of common principles. This approach not only applies to the institutional mobility of IBCs, but also the broader issues of student, staff, and program mobility across international borders.

Several transnational quality assurance efforts have been directly or indirectly in response to negotiations surrounding the General Agreement on Trade in Services (GATS). GATS contemplated a global trade in higher education with numerous implications for transnational recognition of credentials and institutions. An effort by the Global Alliance for Transnational Education to take the lead at the outset of GATS talks in 1995 collapsed within a couple of years when the organization was taken over by a for-profit education corporation (Uvalić-Trumbić 2007). Even though no global agreements on education were ever reached through GATS, and negotiations are now permanently stalled, it continued to be cited through the end of the 2000s as a motivating impulse for quality assurance reforms.

Along with GATS, another significant motivating force for transnational quality assurance has been the Bologna process in Europe. Bologna envisioned the creation of a European higher education area, and proposed the development of common standards that would facilitate the movement of students and faculty across borders. After Bologna, the European Association for Quality Assurance in Higher Education (ENQA) emerged in 2000 as a regional network of national quality assurance agencies, and assumed a leading role in identifying standards and guidelines for quality assurance in the region (Ala-Vähälä and Saarinen 2009). The goal was to develop a common quality framework that could verify the equivalency of credentials earned in any member country.

Taking a different tack, the European University Association (EUA), organized in 2001, argued that new forms of transnational quality assurance should be led by universities (Association of European Universities, 2001). Their concern was that a regional approach as envisioned by Bologna or implied by GATS would ignore institutional diversity and autonomy in favor of a single agency enforcing a common set of standards. The debate was not ignored in the United States, where the Council for Higher Education Accreditation (CHEA) was also concerned about the emerging influence of international organizations in quality assurance, including the ongoing GATS negotiations. As an association of accrediting organizations, CHEA argued that quality assurance leaders as well as leaders of higher education institutions could form an "international confederation" to develop procedures to scrutinize the cross-border delivery of education (Eaton 2003).

The culmination of this line of argument was a 2005 joint statement by CHEA, International Association of Universities (IAU), the Association of Universities and Colleges of Canada (AUCC), and the American Council on Education (ACE) entitled "Sharing Quality Higher Education Across Borders: A Statement on Behalf of Higher Education Institutions Worldwide." The statement clearly put universities at the top of the quality assurance hierarchy, and insisted that international agreements respect national self-regulation of higher education. At the same time, it argued for universities to work within their national and international associations to develop appropriate quality assurance principles and apply them to cross-border higher education.

A parallel effort to address issues of cross-border quality assurance was being led by UNESCO. Several forums on international quality assurance

62   MULTINATIONAL COLLEGES AND UNIVERSITIES

were sponsored by UNESCO in the early 2000s, which eventually resulted in "Guidelines for Quality Provision in Cross-Border Higher Education" (UNESCO 2005). In contrast to the associations' joint statement, UNESCO placed governments at the head of the table, recommending every country make transparent progress toward the development of regulations for licensing of foreign campuses at home, and developing procedures for quality assurance for the provision of cross-border higher education by their own domestic institutions.

Meanwhile ENQA continued its role as the quality assurance advisor for the Bologna process. The development of common and enforceable quality standards proved difficult, especially in the face of fairly widespread opposition as suggested by the UNESCO and associations' statements. Moreover, ENQA accepted EUA involvement in the development of a report that outlined recommendations for quality assurance in the European higher education area (ENQA 2005). Rather than developing a monolithic approach to quality assurance, the recommendations emphasize first, the primacy of internal institutional quality assurance, and second, respect for the national quality assurance regimes already in existence. It develops standards for what internal and external quality assurance should accomplish, rather than dictate how quality assurance should be done. It also sets forth guidelines for quality assurance agencies to ensure they are professional, credible, and allow for international comparability and acceptance.

This last role, of establishing guidelines for quality assurance agencies, led to the development of the European Quality Assurance Register for Higher Education. The register includes any quality assurance agency from a member state of the European Higher Education Area that applies to be listed in the register and meets the standards set forth by ENQA. Currently, the register is simply a list of recognized agencies. But the goal is to build trust in the quality standards employed across Europe such that national regulations will allow institutions to choose among registered agencies.

One final multinational quality assurance effort deserves mention. The International Network for Quality Assurance Agencies in Higher Education (INQAAHE) encourages the development of regional networks of quality assurance agencies, governments, and other interested parties, and seeks to coordinate inter-regional cooperation. INQAAHE currently recognizes eleven regional associations, including ones from Africa, Asia, the Caribbean, Europe, the Middle East, and South and Central America. Notably absent from any of these networks is North America.

Conclusion

All of the current efforts at multinational quality assurance have developed since 2000, suggesting widespread recognition of a common problem. Yet no solution has emerged to dominate current discussions. In fact, as Uvalić-Trumbić (2007) states, "There is a growing tension between perceiving the quality of higher education solely as an issue for sovereign nation-states and the increasing calls for and attempts at international accreditation schemes" (p. 59). The current system operates largely on a buyer-beware model, requiring importing countries to always be on guard against substandard operations. The regional networks and the cooperation encouraged by the European register are positive developments, as are innovative approaches such as the QAA's country audits, or UQAIB's endorsement of adequate home-country evaluation. But they still grant sovereignty to geopolitical entities (Kinser 2009). Until the extent of cross-border trust matches that of cross-border higher education, a truly multinational quality assurance regime remains hypothetical.

References

Ala-Vähälä, T., and T. Saarinen. 2009. "Building European-Level Quality Assurance Structures: Views from Within ENQA." *Quality in Higher Education* 15 (2): 89–103.

Association of European Universities. 2001. *Towards Accreditation Schemes for Higher Education in Europe?* Paris: Association of European Universities.

Australian Universities Quality Agency [AUQA]. 2008. *TNE Quality Framework of AUQA.* Melbourne: Australian Universities Quality Agency.

CHEA, IAU, AUCC, and ACE. 2005. Sharing Quality Higher Education Across Borders: A Statement on Behalf of Higher Education Institutions Worldwide. Washington, DC: Authors.

Cheung, P.P.T. 2006. "Filleting the Transnational Education Steak." *Quality in Higher Education* 12 (3): 283–285.

Eaton, J. S. (2003). *Do We Need an International Confederation for Quality Review of Higher Education?* Washington, DC: Council for Higher Education Accreditation.

ENQA. 2005. *Standards and Guidelines for Quality Assurance in the European Higher Education Area.* Helsinki: European Association for Quality Assurance in Higher Education.

Harvey, L. 2005. "A History and Critique of Quality Evaluation in the UK." *Quality Assurance in Education* 13 (4): 263–276.

Harvey, L. 2011. *Analytic Quality Glossary.* Quality Research International (online). Available at www.qualityresearchinternational.com/glossary/. Accessed February 25, 2011.

Jackson, S. 2006. "The Quality Assurance of Transnational Education: The UK experience of QAA Overseas Audit." In J. Baird (ed.), *Quality Audit and Assurance for Transnational Higher Education* (pp. 11–20). Melbourne: Australian Universities Quality Agency.

Kinser, K. 2009, December 13. "Liberalisation, Quality, and Profit: Tensions in Cross Border Delivery of Higher Education." Paper presented at the Global Higher Education Forum. Penang, Malaysia.

Kinser, K. 2010. "A Global Perspective on For-Profit Higher Education." In *Learning for Earning in a Globalized Society: For-profit Colleges and Universities as Schools and Businesses*, edited by William G. Tierney, Vicente M. Lechuga, and Guilbert Hentschke, 145–170. Sterling, VA: Stylus Press.

Kinser, K., and B. A. Hill. In press. *Higher Education in Turbulent Times: Facing Market Forces—Promoting the Common Good.* Washington, DC: American Council on Education.

Kinser, K., D. C. Levy, J. C. Silas Casillas, A. Bernasconi, S. Slantcheva-Durst, W. Otieno, et al. 2010. "The Global Growth of Private Higher Education." *ASHE Higher Education Report* 36 (3). San Francisco: Jossey-Bass.

64 MULTINATIONAL COLLEGES AND UNIVERSITIES

Kristoffersen, D. 2006. "AUQA's Approach to Auditing Transnational Education." In *Quality Audit and Assurance for Transnational Higher Education*, edited by J. Baird, 1–9. Melbourne: Australian Universities Quality Agency.

Lane, J. E. 2010. *Higher Education, Free Zones, and Quality Assurance in Dubai*. Policy Paper. Dubai: Dubai School of Government.

Lewis, R. 2009. "Quality Assurance in Higher Education—Its Global Future." In OECD (ed.), *Higher Education to 2030, Volume 2, Globalisation* (pp. 323–355). Paris: OECD Publishing.

McBurnie, G., and C. Ziguras. 2007. *Transnational Education: Issues and Trends in Offshore Higher Education*. London: Routledge.

Principles of Good Practice in Overseas International Education Programs for Non-U.S. Nationals. 1997. Bedford, MA: New England Association of Schools and Colleges Commission on Institutions of Higher Education.

Quality Assurance Agency for Higher Education. 2011. "Overseas Audit Reports" (online). Available at www.qaa.ac.uk/reviews/reports/byoseascountry.asp. Accessed February 25, 2011.

Quality Assurance Agency. 2010. *Code of Practice for the Assurance of Academic Quality and Standards in Higher Education, Section 2: Collaborative Provision and Flexible and Distributed Learning (Including E-learning)*. Gloucester: Quality Assurance Agency for Higher Education.

Rawazik, W., and M. Carroll. 2009. "Complexity in Quality Assurance in a Rapidly Growing Free Economic Environment: A UAE Case Study." *Quality in Higher Education* 15 (1): 79–83.

Sanyal, B. C., and M. Martin. 2007. "Quality Assurance and the Role of Accreditation: An Overview." In Global University Network for Innovation (ed.), *Higher Education in the World 2007: Accreditation for Quality Assurance: What Is at Stake?* (pp. 3–17). New York: Palgrave Macmillan.

UNESCO. 2005. *Guidelines for Quality Provision in Cross-Border Higher Education*. Paris: United Nations Educational, Scientific and Cultural Organization.

Universities UK. (2008). *Quality and Standards in UK Universities: A Guide to How the System Works*. London: Author.

Uvalić-Trumbić, S. 2007. "The International Politics of Quality Assurance and Accreditation: From Legal Instruments to Communities of Practice." In Global University Network for Innovation (ed.), *Higher Education in the World 2007: Accreditation for Quality Assurance: What Is at Stake?* (pp. 58–72). New York: Palgrave Macmillan.

van Ginkel, H.J.A., and M.A.R. Dias. 2007. "Institutional and Political Challenges of Accreditation at the International Level." In Global University Network for Innovation (ed.), *Higher Education in the World 2007: Accreditation for Quality Assurance: What Is at Stake?* (pp. 37–57). New York: Palgrave Macmillan.

Woodhouse, D. (2006). "The Quality of Transnational Education: A Provider View." *Quality in Higher Education* 12 (3): 277–281.

KEVIN KINSER is an Associate Professor, Senior Researcher at the Institute for Global Education Policy Studies, State University of New York, Albany. He co-leads the Cross-Border Education Research Team (www.globalhighered.org).

This chapter provides specific advice for how IBCs can negotiate entry into a foreign legal environment and operate support systems that can coordinate the management operations on multiple campuses.

Operational Considerations for Opening a Branch Campus Abroad

Lawrence M. Harding, Robert W. Lammey

Spring 2014 will mark the graduation of the first four-year class of New York University's Abu Dhabi campus, approximately seven years since fifteen faculty and administrators from NYU traveled nearly 7,000 miles to the emirate state from their home campus in New York City to discuss building a local campus with the United Arab Emirates (UAE) government.

NYU clearly understood the importance of academic and operational planning long before the NYU Abu Dhabi campus became a physical reality. In 2006, representatives of NYU and the emirate of Abu Dhabi met and recognized a partnership between the government of Abu Dhabi and the university. An agreement was reached a year later, when both parties committed to building a US-style, research-focused educational institution. NYU Abu Dhabi, a residential research university, would be an international branch campus (IBC) of NYU New York, operated consistently with NYU New York's academic quality and practices. The inaugural class of 188 students began courses as the construction of the campus was still being finalized, underscoring a long planning process that kicked off with the initial request of $50 million from UAE investors.

The NYU example serves as an object lesson for other schools contemplating international expansion. Universities have been attracted to the creation of IBCs for many reasons, including cultural immersion of students and faculty and global brand recognition for a university seeking to enhance its reputation and strengthen its academic standards (McBurnie and Ziguras 2007; Naidoo 2009). In this chapter, we discuss some common approaches to successfully opening a university presence abroad, particularly for an endeavor as significant as an IBC. This includes:

NEW DIRECTIONS FOR HIGHER EDUCATION, no. 155, Fall 2011 © Wiley Periodicals, Inc.
Published online in Wiley Online Library (wileyonlinelibrary.com) • DOI:10.1002/he.445

66   MULTINATIONAL COLLEGES AND UNIVERSITIES

- Understanding the local culture and expectations of the government.
- Engaging academic and administrative leadership early in the process.
- Establishing employee hiring and retention practices to address cultural values and differences.
- Establishing adequate budgets and timelines.

Overseeing foreign operations can create challenges for any organization, but branch campuses pose a unique set of challenges for universities. Establishing a campus in a foreign country requires college and university officials to adapt institutional business operations to meet cultural, legal, and environmental conditions very different from those at the home campus, an endeavor that entails much more than operating academic programs that transcend international borders. Institutions must negotiate entry into a foreign legal environment and operate support systems that help facilitate the implementation of expansion plans, establishment of appropriate legal entities, employment of personnel, establishment of payment procedures for overseas faculty and staff, all while ensuring appropriate navigation of overseas tax codes and compliance regulations. Drawing on the experience of the authors in helping universities expand into overseas markets, this chapter provides readers with detailed information about how to handle the challenges associated with opening an IBC.

Initial Challenges and Considerations

In order to assert a strong institutional presence in a foreign location, colleges and universities must ensure that geographic distance does not inhibit effective oversight of such an operation (see chapters 1 and 2 for additional discussion of internal oversight issues). It will be important to consider, during the operational planning, how an IBC would be overseen by responsible officials from the university—academically, financially, and culturally—on the understanding that such activities should be no less integral a part of a university than activities based in the home country. The potential complexities of operating an overseas campus may well mean that officials from the home campus should expect to devote more attention to their oversight than to comparable operations based at home; however, some studies have found that institutional leaders are sometimes less engaged in such activities at the IBC than on the home campus (see, e.g., Coleman 2003; Lane 2010).

There should be clarity from the outset about the substance and scope of any specific proposal to extend a university's presence to locations remote from a home campus and a clear awareness of potential risk. Common concerns associated with expansion include:

- The physical safety of faculty and students who spend anywhere from a few days to several years in foreign countries.
- The protection of a university's name and identity.

NEW DIRECTIONS FOR HIGHER EDUCATION • DOI:10.1002/he

OPERATIONAL CONSIDERATIONS FOR OPENING A BRANCH CAMPUS ABROAD   67

- The compliance of a university and its agents with the operating and employment laws, regulations, and customs of foreign jurisdictions.
- The management of operational logistics in remote locations.
- Adherence to the high standards of accountability that have been established over many decades by the university on its home campus.

As a university begins its planning at home for the prospect of a branch campus abroad, academic leadership of the university will often begin immediately the arduous task of developing a scholastic curriculum that will maintain the high standards which the university has endeavored to establish since its inception. The decentralized governance typical of higher education can pose some peculiar challenges, but as universities increasingly reach beyond their own boundaries, they must coordinate their activities effectively in order to harness shared strengths from different corners of the institution, and realize efficiencies wherever possible. This is especially true for an endeavor as significant as establishing a degree-granting campus in a foreign country.

NYU first organized faculty and administration committees to develop the general contours of the curriculum, followed a year later by six coordinating committees in the areas of Arts, Economics and Finance, Engineering, Humanities, Sciences, and Social Sciences. The coordinating committees developed detailed curriculum and began faculty recruitment, while working closely with the departments, units, and schools of the university.

Understanding Local Laws

Understanding the laws governing the provision of educational services in the country being contemplated for a branch is important, as federal or provincial laws often exist that require the university to partner in some capacity with a local institution, whether to grant actual degrees, or carry out other educational programs (Kinser et al. 2010; McBurnie and Ziguras 2007). Understanding the expectations of the local government regarding involvement by a local institution must be engaged early, to ensure the independence necessary to achieve the desired standard of academic excellence. Such details concerning development and control over the curriculum should be addressed during the early negotiations with local authorities. Ongoing control of the curriculum for the life of the campus operation should also be agreed.

Additional consideration must also be given to a foreign government's objectives for offering educational opportunities to local residents versus the university's objectives for enhancing the student experience for those enrolled in the home campus. This may apply for faculty as well as students. Admission standards for all students of the campus abroad, especially those of the local country, must be established and agreed to with the foreign authorities during the negotiation of the contemplated campus.

68   MULTINATIONAL COLLEGES AND UNIVERSITIES

Faculty recruitment for an overseas campus should also be a part of the planning process for an overseas branch campus (see also chapter 2). In addition to the appointment of faculty from the home campus as part of the setup and planning phase, the hiring of faculty for an overseas campus may often target academics to be hired locally, whether on a permanent basis or (as is often the case) on a short-term or trial basis, and will typically include a mix of local and nonlocal (expatriate) hires. Controls and guidelines over the hiring process should be developed that mirror the standards for faculty and administrative staff hiring on the home campus. This is important due to hiring practice differences that may exist between cultures. For example, hiring decisions in some countries often favor family and friends due to perceived trustworthiness, while in other cultures relatives are barred from employment. Resources on the home campus established to maintain standards that may need to be adapted for recruitment of faculty and staff on an overseas campus may include items such as:

- Faculty and staff recruitment handbooks.
- A faculty recruitment committee.
- Links to professional societies in the foreign country including professional societies geared toward minority and women's interests.
- Information from independent government agencies established to promote educational resources in that country.
- Guide to acceptable interview questions.
- Sample candidate evaluation templates.

Promotion and ongoing performance evaluation practices should also be contemplated early to avoid possible tensions between leadership and locally hired staff. As an example, promotions in some cultures are often based on loyalties to a superior, while in other cultures promotion is based strictly on performance. Also, a formal feedback process, now standard in many Western countries, is still not fully accepted in all cultures. Locally hired employees may be sensitive to giving and receiving critical feedback, whereas many Western cultures universally accept and practice critical feedback. Employee manuals and expectation-setting for performance management will help ensure that these differences do not become a distraction to the academic purpose of the overseas campus in the first years of operation.

Closely related to hiring standards, a clear understanding of local laws and customs must also be included in discussions with a foreign partner about the values that will dictate the hiring and ongoing social and ethical guidelines of the campus. Any planning to create an overseas presence must ensure due attention to the local laws, regulations, and customs that may bear upon institutional activities conducted elsewhere. Absent these considerations, tensions may emerge between local laws or customs and the university's own policies and academic values with respect to such matters as nondiscrimination against individuals; expectations regarding academic freedom; and the appropriate relationship between a university and its members, on the one hand, and various public and private institutions, on the other. Whether and how such potential tensions can be resolved may reflect significantly on the merits of the adequacy of the planning process.

For example, NYU and its Abu Dhabi partners developed a statement of shared values (http://nyuad.nyu.edu/about/labour.values.html) applicable to individuals who built and ultimately staffed NYU Abu Dhabi. This statement set forth standards and expectations for the appropriate treatment of individuals building and staffing NYU Abu Dhabi, and set forth guidelines about items such as (but not limited to) compensation, living conditions, workplace safety, and working conditions like hours and rest periods. The cultural considerations must be carefully evaluated and contemplated due to everyday differences that may exist with the culture and values of the home country. As an example, many countries in the Middle East and in parts of Southeast Asia and northern Africa recognize a standard workweek as Sunday through Thursday. Local religious customs often can dictate fundamental differences between cultures that must be considered when planning a campus abroad, particularly in the context of students and faculty who may be present on the overseas campus. (See chapter 1 for further discussion.)

Other, less tangible cultural differences should also be taken into consideration, even in the context of the discussions and negotiations themselves. Many cultures value etiquette and manners as a measure of respect, including when eating meals and even during negotiations in a business meetings, while other cultures often sacrifice formality for efficiency in a "Let's get to the point" approach.

Policies and Ongoing Governance

The infrastructure of the overseas campus should strive to mirror the structure that a university has in its home country in many ways. The formation of policies and process from the outset will establish a foundation of guidelines that will shape the strength of the campus infrastructure. Policies are important for the promotion of:

- Consistent and fair practice across all departments and schools.
- Compliance with laws and regulations.
- Management of costs.
- Safety for employees and students.

To the extent policies already exist in the home country, many would likely be applicable or require only minor modification for the overseas campus. In certain cases, policies should be reviewed for consistency with local laws and regulations, as the home country laws may be quite different.

70   MULTINATIONAL COLLEGES AND UNIVERSITIES

An example would be the hiring of contractors, whereby employee-contractor classification laws can differ from country to country. As an example, in Russia an individual must be formally registered and approved to provide services on a contract basis. Even once classified correctly as a contractor, the withholding requirements and year-end reporting requirements may be very different from that of the home country. Understanding the differences in local laws from the home country is of critical importance in establishing policies with an overseas campus.

Examples of policies that may require some modification but otherwise should be similar to existing policies at the home campus include:

- Travel policy (tends to address short-term trips and required documentation for reimbursement).
- Transaction and contract authority.
- Personnel management and performance review process.
- University-owned assets.

Examples of policies that may be unique to an overseas campus or other international activity, or require more significant modification from the home policy, include:

- Global mobility and immigration practices (secondments, local employees, and longer-term business trips).
- Governance policy.
- Health and safety.
- Export compliance.
- Donations to foreign sites.
- Hedging foreign currency risk.
- Hiring of contractors.

Operational Planning in a Foreign Country

Adequate operational planning is paramount to the ultimate achievement of the long-term objectives and must be commenced early to allow for the academic development of the campus abroad to ultimately achieve its goals and standards. Challenges in the planning of a campus are increased in countries that speak a different language and with significantly different time zones. Considerations for "on-the-ground" management of the campus increase with both of these factors present.

There are numerous operational planning considerations that need to be completed before the first students set foot on the new campus. Quite often, years of effective project management are required to successfully complete the operational infrastructure necessary to begin safe and effective academic activities. Cultural differences should also be considered in the planning of campus construction, with local interpretation of target milestones and

OPERATIONAL CONSIDERATIONS FOR OPENING A BRANCH CAMPUS ABROAD   71

deadlines being relatively conceptual rather than literally imperative. Budgeting should provide for the possibility of missed deadlines, as the delay of educational activities can result in an entire year of missed revenue while cost commitments remain firm.

Temporary infrastructure is necessary prior to the groundbreaking of the campus construction itself, and in fact, for most overseas locations, an actual physical address for local operations is required before any legal presence in-country will be approved. One approach is to think about activities that require one-time setup versus those that will be ongoing after the campus opens for business. Many of the one-time items may need to be revisited on an annual or biannual basis, but generally won't need ongoing attention. Examples of one-time setup items include:

- Planning and campus development budget.
- Legal entity determination and registration.
- Facilities planning and procurement (design and construction).
- Emergency preparedness plan (evacuation).
- Business continuity and disaster recovery plans.
- Bank selection and accounts.
- Insurance.
- Hiring (may be phased over first few years).
- Compensation and benefits practices.
- Policy development.

Examples of ongoing planning considerations include:

- Annual budget.
- Campus security.
- Dining services.
- Procurement (ongoing campus operations).
- Cultural training (for incoming students each year).
- Facilities management (buildings).
- Grounds/landscaping.
- Back-office support (financial and compliance).
- Information technology (IT).
- Student services.
- Health services.
- Research compliance (local).
- Financial aid and student loans.

The overseas campus must comply with numerous local, provincial, and federal laws and regulations. Engaging the assistance of local attorneys, accountants, and other business advisors is good practice during the initial planning, particularly when language differences may prove challenging for home-country university attorneys and administrators.

72 MULTINATIONAL COLLEGES AND UNIVERSITIES

Regulatory Matters

Early in the planning phase, it is important to reach out and build relationships with the local, municipal, provincial, and federal officials involved with where the campus plans to locate. Examples of local considerations are zoning, parking, sign regulations, certain occupational licenses, and, in many countries (China prominently, for example), the actual name approval for local operations. Permission must also be granted in many countries and local jurisdictions to conduct educational activities. Requirements for licenses to conduct educational activities would often be addressed during the initial discussions with the local authorities.

Corporate Taxes. When determining the most advantageous legal entity with which to establish the overseas campus, it is important to understand the varying forms of standard and not-for-profit entity structures in the foreign country. Certain countries do not recognize nonprofit entities, and a standard for-profit entity type may be necessary even though the educational activity itself may not be taxable. As there may be varying forms of income generated with the overseas campus, including executive education, sales of educational books and publications, fund-raising, and numerous forms of educational-related activities (food sales, parking fees, etc.), it is important to understand the various tax implications for all activities. Whether generating income or simply related to revenues (turnover) or transactions (value-added tax [VAT], for example), the local tax ramifications may be very different overseas from the tax treatments in the home country.

Insurance. Many business and employee benefits types of insurances are mandatory by law. Where not compulsory, it is important to understand which business insurances represent best practice, and for employee benefits, which types of incremental coverage would be "expected" by employees of a similar role working for a similar organization.

Environmental Issues. There may be complex air-quality requirements or waste disposal regulations to consider and ensure compliance with. For example, in the European Union, the Waste Electrical and Electronic Equipment (WEEE) and Restriction of Hazardous Substances (RoHS) directives are intended to address financial and other responsibilities with regard to the collection and recycling of waste, along with banning the use of certain hazardous substances, mainly for companies selling electrical goods in the EU. However, the compliance requirements impact many other types of operations and would certainly come into play related to an overseas branch campus. This is an area of frequently changing laws, so establishing a process of understanding laws and future proposed changes is good practice during campus planning.

Home-Country Compliance

There are filings and registrations that may be impacted or required due to the commencement of activities outside a home country. These generally range from additional information required on a tax return to specific filings of information that are required only if there are activities outside the home country. Using the United States as an example, there are several domestic forms, filings, and laws that must be considered when opening a campus abroad. Some of these include:

Tax Requirements. IRS Form 990, Schedule F—501(c)(3) organizations must provide information on their annual tax returns related to activities conducted by the organization outside the United States at any time during the tax year. Reportable activities include grant making; fund-raising activities; unrelated trade or business; program services; passive investments; or maintaining offices, employees, or agents for the purpose of conducting any such activities in regions outside the United States. The operations of an overseas branch campus would certainly be reportable.

Report of Foreign Bank and Financial Accounts (FBAR). Institutions are typically required to report certain bank account information and activity if the aggregate value of these accounts exceeds $10,000 at any time during the calendar year, which is an extremely low threshold. In addition to a filing on behalf of the institution, individual employees who meet the definition of a US person and have signatory authority over an institution's bank account in a foreign country must also file a report as an individual. The individual filing requirements have been a topic of much discussion, and current requirements should be verified by visiting the IRS website or working with the institution's tax advisor.

Export Control Regulations. US federal law prohibits the unlicensed export of certain commodities or information, for reasons of national security. Export controls usually arise if the nature of the export has military applications or economic protection issues, or if there may be government concerns about the intended use, destination country, organization, or end user of the export. An export is any oral, written, electronic, or visual disclosure, shipment, transfer, or transmission of commodities, technology, information, technical data, assistance, or software codes to anyone outside the United States, including a US citizen, a non-US individual, or a foreign embassy or affiliate. In the higher ed space, examples of typical "Technology Transfer" mechanisms where export control requirements must be adhered to can include scientific, engineering, and academic exchanges; international meetings or symposia; and even simply general "international visits."

Examples of other considerations for US institutions with activities abroad include:

- Office of Foreign Asset Control (OFAC) compliance.
- Clery Act.
- Foreign Corrupt Practices Act.
- Human subject research compliance.
- Animal care.

74   MULTINATIONAL COLLEGES AND UNIVERSITIES

Employment Matters

An overseas campus may be required to establish safety and health programs and to minimize hazards to prevent workplace injuries and illnesses. Safety requirements vary greatly from country to country, including such topics as fire exits, sprinklers and detectors, and even workplace poster requirements.

Local laws addressing civil rights protections to individuals with disabilities similar to those provided to individuals on the basis of race, color, sex, national origin, age, and religion may exist and are different country to country. These may guarantee equal opportunity for individuals with disabilities in campus accommodations, employment, on-campus transportation, and telecommunications.

Prior to the employment of local staff and administrators, obtain information on how to comply with federal and local employment laws that relate to wages, health, and other employee benefits, retirement security, and employment rights. There are typically cases where an employee is subject to both local and federal minimum wage laws, work hours, and benefit plans. Offering benefits that may be more than what is required by local law is often a powerful recruitment and retention tool, but it may be economically disadvantageous. It is important to understand both statutory requirements and culturally expected benefits and compensation levels prior to engaging in local hiring.

Employment of local nationals will likely play a large role in the planning and ongoing support of a campus abroad. Senior faculty and key administrators to campus security maintenance will likely be hired from the outset of campus planning until soon before the first students set foot on the new grounds, with natural turnover and planned growth in the first few years also requiring the ongoing process of hiring.

Employment contracts in writing are usually a requirement in foreign countries, but documenting all employment relationships—full-time employees, part-time employees, and contractors—is also good business practice to protect the interests of the university against misunderstandings of terms and potential legal proceedings upon termination.

Employment contracts are only one of the major labor issues universities face when conducting activities abroad. Terminating a local national employee can also create major problems, since outside the United States the concept of "employment at will" rarely exists. Like employment contracts, there are strict procedures and processes for terminating employees that vary by country. There can be heavy monetary penalties if terminations are handled improperly, as settlements are usually calculated as a multiple of annual earnings. As an example, in the EU, termination settlements can amount to two to three years of earnings, but settlements as high as eight times earnings have also been noted, depending on the severity of a breach by the employer in the eyes of a local court.

NEW DIRECTIONS FOR HIGHER EDUCATION • DOI:10.1002/he

Understanding legal and statutory requirements for compensation, benefits, and labor laws is also important. This will help ensure that the university is compliant with local employment requirements while also ensuring the highest morale of its local employees. There is also likely to be a number of employees from the home country who are assigned, or seconded, to an overseas campus as expatriates. Having home-country employees seconded to an overseas campus can help ensure that academic standards are being met and maintained, and that other desired aspects of the home campus culture and standards are being transferred to the overseas campus. However, expatriate assignments typically cost the employer between two and three times the annual salary earned by the US employee assigned, and in many locations the US-only salary for the position can be higher than the local national equivalent in the first place.

Best practice is to set a standard policy for "assignment-related compensation," providing clarity to expatriate employees and employers, with clearly defined terms and equality of treatment between employees. Local laws and customs relate differently to local nationals, expatriates, third-country nationals (meaning, in the case of a US university, a citizen of one foreign country who is working for the university in a different foreign country), and contractors. For all categories of employees, there should be an understanding of what benefits are mandatory in the foreign country, then what incrementally would be "market norm." Comparison with the home-country benefit plan can certainly be a factor in evaluating local benefits, but it shouldn't be the only one or even the most important one.

Examples of local laws and customs that may apply include:

- Work hours, overtime, and other premium pay.
- Unions and works councils.
- Paid time off and unpaid leaves.
- Privacy.
- Bonuses and employer subsidies.
- Nondiscrimination, harassment, retaliation.
- Dismissals and severance.
- Occupational safety.

The hiring of contractors is common practice in higher education for programs abroad, due to the reduced administrative burden, but it also carries the most risk. The threshold for what constitutes a "valid" contractor is much higher than many imagine, and there are heavy incentives for local authorities to deem contractors as *de facto employees*. Many countries are taking aggressive measures to identify illegal contractor working arrangements, as well as providing incentives for contractors to "blow the whistle" when employers are not properly treating them as the employees they actually should be under local employment laws. Violating these laws can result in heavy penalties and fines from the local government, as well as employment

76   MULTINATIONAL COLLEGES AND UNIVERSITIES

claims from the contractor that may result in a generous settlement. Even properly classified contractors may have withholding and year-end reporting requirements that are different from the home country's, which must be adhered to.

Ongoing Back-Office Support

Not to be underestimated is the importance of establishing a sound infrastructure for the back-office support functions. With the onset of academic development and negotiation with local officials, it will be necessary for local support from the earliest stages of planning. It will likely be necessary to approach back-office support in two phases, with first establishing a temporary structure to support the heavy procurement, hiring, and frequent travelers from the home country while facility planning and construction are at their highest levels. As the campus development moves into its more mature phases and begins to prepare for the arrival of students, a different structure to support the long-term operations of the campus may need to be implemented.

Examples of typical back-office functions for an overseas campus include:

- Payroll services, including monthly, quarterly, and annual compliance and statutory filings for local employees, expatriates, and third-country nationals.
- Bookkeeping management services, including posting all required vouchers and journal entries, filing all invoices and bank account statements, preparation and review of financial statements in compliance with local requirements, and retaining other supporting documentation in accordance with proper office administration.
- Accounts Payable (A/P) processing services.
- Employee expense report processing services.
- Student billing and collection.
- Cash management services, including the coordination of all required payments in-country—net payroll, payroll taxes, employee expense reimbursements, A/P, and other supplier payments as required.
- Completion of management accounts and submission back to home-country financial administration of a monthly reporting package (which typically would include a balance sheet, statement of income and expenses, trial balance, general ledger, fixed-asset register, balance sheet reconciliations, and an intercompany service invoice for the month) in accordance with local accounting requirements and in local currency.
- Monthly funding of the entity if not supported by local student tuition and donations.
- Preparation, filing, and coordinating payment of relevant statutory taxes as appropriate for the form of local registration.

Partnering with Local Institutions

As previously mentioned, many countries have laws in place that prohibit outside institutions from conducting educational activities without the involvement of a local educational institution, which may also be affiliated with the foreign government (Lane 2010; McBurnie and Ziguras 2007). There can be many benefits of partnering with a local institution, whether required by law or not. In addition to accelerated opportunities for educational programs for students, partners can help introduce a foreign university to the local culture through shared programs, exchange agreements for faculty and students, and even introductions to local government officials who may be influential as a foreign institution looks to advance its interests of having a campus in that country.

Risks associated with partnering also require careful consideration, with the most prevalent being control over academic curriculum, use of the university's name by the partner institution, and use of shared space when not being used for educational purposes (see Dunworth 2008; Lane 2010; see also chapter 5 in this volume). It's often good practice to begin a partner relationship with small endeavors such as short student trips with the partner institution or even a summer school program before engaging in longer-term initiatives such as a joint-degree program or exchange of students and faculty in a long-term agreement. This allows both parties to get to know each other first, and can introduce each to its own cultural values and customs to establish the basis for something more permanent.

The expectations of each party to a partnership should be thoroughly discussed and documented as much as possible in a memorandum of understanding between the two parties. Obtaining assistance from local counsel to assist in the drafting of such an agreement is important since contract law varies greatly country to country. Considerations of administrative support items to include in a memorandum of understanding might include:

- Protocol for hiring and terminating mutual local employees.
- Upkeep and management of mutually used administrative and classroom space.
- Paying of vendors.
- Procurement process for purchase of goods and services.
- Invoicing and collection (if applicable).
- IT support and security, as well as disaster recovery.
- Insurance coverage over shared facilities and assets.

Conclusion

The excitement of opening a campus abroad should help bring together the academic and administrative leadership in a planning effort focused on

78 MULTINATIONAL COLLEGES AND UNIVERSITIES

the operational planning effort necessary to achieve a successful branch campus abroad. Key takeaways from this chapter include:

- Understand the local culture and expectations of local officials before agreeing on a partnership with a foreign government.
- Engage academic and administrative leadership early on the home campus to enable mutual success.
- Establish employee hiring and retention practices that will address cultural values and potential differences on the campus abroad.
- Establish adequate budgets and project timelines to ensure timely commencement of student tuition revenue streams and overall financial success.

References

Coleman, D. 2003. "Quality Assurance in Transnational Education." *Journal of Studies in International Education* 7 (4): 354–378.

Dunworth, K. 2008. "Ideas and Realities: Investigating Good Practice in the Management of Transnational English Language Programmes for the Higher Education Sector." *Quality in Higher Education* 14 (2): 95–107.

Kinser, K., D. C. Levy, J. C. Silas Casillas, A. Bernasconi, S. Slantcheva-Durst, W. Otieno, et al. 2010. "The Global Growth of Private Higher Education." *ASHE Higher Education Report* 36 (3). San Francisco: Jossey-Bass.

Lane, J. E. 2010. "Joint Ventures in Cross-Border Higher Education: International Branch Campuses in Malaysia." In *Cross Border Collaborations in Higher Education: Partnerships Beyond the Classroom,* edited by D. W. Chapman and R. Sakamoto, 67–90. New York: Routledge.

McBurnie, G., and C. Ziguras. 2007. *Transnational Education: Issues and Trends in Offshore Higher Education.* New York: Routledge.

Naidoo, J. 2009. "Transnational Higher Education: A Stock Taking of Current Activity." *Journal of Studies in International Education* 13 (3): 310–330.

LAWRENCE M. HARDING is the President and Founder of High Street Partners, a business services firm specializing in helping organizations internationalize their operations.

ROBERT W. LAMMEY is the Director of Higher Education at High Street Partners, a business services firm specializing in helping organizations internationalize their operations.

7 *Policies for importing and exporting international branch campuses are increasingly being formalized, with a number of countries explicitly encouraging educational trade as an economic development goal.*

The Cross-Border Education Policy Context: Educational Hubs, Trade Liberalization, and National Sovereignty

Jason E. Lane, Kevin Kinser

Introduction

International branch campuses (IBCs) operate in national and international policy environments that are still rapidly evolving. While IBCs have been operating for several decades, most of that time they have operated below the domestic regulatory radar of either the exporting (home) or importing (host) governments. As the number of such institutions has increased, both home and host governments are beginning to pay more attention to the development of such institutions. As Kinser points out in chapter 5, home governments have a desire to preserve the quality and reputation of the home campus, while host governments are primarily interested in ensuring that a quality academic program is provided at the IBC. Thus, in the absence of international treaties regulating the flow of educational services, IBCs tend to exist at crossroads of policy arenas.

The idea of a unified cross-border education policy arena is somewhat of a misnomer. There is an emerging discourse focused on the movement of educational institutions across borders, and several regional organizations have emerged to encourage geographically proximate countries to operate under a common education policy umbrella. However, there has yet to emerge a powerful supranational educational policy framework or organization, and the locus of power remains with the nation-state.

Multinational colleges and universities inherently operate in multinational policy arenas; the nature of those arenas changes, depending on where the institutions have a presence. Though the locus of power remains

NEW DIRECTIONS FOR HIGHER EDUCATION, no. 155, Fall 2011 © Wiley Periodicals, Inc.
Published online in Wiley Online Library (wileyonlinelibrary.com) • DOI:10.1002/he.446

80   MULTINATIONAL COLLEGES AND UNIVERSITIES

with the nation-state, a global perspective is required to fully understand the different policy entanglements in which IBCs operate. It is difficult, though, to understand what is happening within any one policy arena, without some knowledge of the other policy arenas. In part, there is a level of competition at play among some importing and exporting nations and full understanding of what transpires in one policy arena is evident only when compared against another such arena.

The purpose of this chapter is to provide a very brief overview of the emerging policy arenas in which IBCs now operate. The review is meant as an introduction for those unfamiliar with forces driving the development of IBCs, including the desire of some governments to create educational hubs. For additional information about the policies, politics, or propaganda pertaining to the importing or exporting of educational institutions, see the publications summarized in the annotated bibliography (chapter 8).

The Emerging Policy Context

The development of the cross-border policy environment is influenced by the often competing forces of globalization and national sovereignty, and compounded by the creation of new developmental strategies such as educational hubs.

Globalization. The concept of globalization entered the lexicon in the mid-1990s, and its definitions are varied and nuanced. Globalization has been used in both positive and negative ways to describe the "widening, deepening, and speeding up of worldwide interconnectedness" (Held, McGrew, Goldblatt, and Perraton 1999, 2). The nature of the process is debatable, but the increasing global interconnectedness is difficult to deny. Moreover, the IBC policy arena is influenced by globalization through increased liberalization of trade policies and heightened awareness of national competitiveness.

Trade Policies. Over the past two decades there has been an increased global flow of goods and services due to governments reducing trade barriers. Education has proven to be an attractive tradable service. The Singaporean Ministry of Trade and Industry (MTI) estimated the total global education market in 2002 at US$2.2 trillion (MTI 2004), and education is a top export for many countries. According to the US Bureau of Economic Analysis (BEA), education is one of the top ten US service exports, grossing almost US$20 billion in 2009; Australia's Department of Foreign Affairs and Trade reports that education is the leading service export with almost AU$19 billion in 2009.[1]

The original push for liberalization of trade policies came from the World Trade Organization (WTO), which was attempting to promulgate the General Agreement on Trades and Services (GATS). GATS labeled education as a tradable service. While the discussions on GATS have stalled, a number of multinational regional trade agreements were signed and applied

NEW DIRECTIONS FOR HIGHER EDUCATION • DOI:10.1002/he

to educational services. In addition to trade agreements, several nations, believing that they could benefit from the educational services provided by other nations, altered their own trade policies by either eliminating or reducing their restrictions on the ability of foreign education providers to operate degree-granting academic programs within their borders.

National Competitiveness. Globalization has also fostered a heightened competition among nations for economic and political superiority. In many ways, IBCs have emerged as a strategic resource in this competition. For one, there is an increased recognition that higher education is important for the economic development of many nations. Instead of solely relying on strengthening their domestic higher education sector, a process that could take decades, some nations have elected to recruit IBCs as a way to quickly expand capacity and access to academic programs offered by reputable and established colleges and universities in other countries (Lane 2011). Second, the presence of a strong higher education sector can be seen as a way to improve the soft power influence of some governments (Nye 2005). For example, a prestigious institution choosing to open an IBC in a developing nation could be used as a way to signal the legitimization of the importing nation in the international context and increase the nation's ability to recruit foreign students to pursue their studies in the importing nation.

National Sovereignty. Nations are imbued with the highest level of autonomy and authority. The nation is an abstract entity comprised of citizens and usually designated by a specific land or territory. A nation can set its own policies and establish its own governing structure. Not even supranational organizations such as the United Nations are supposed to violate national sovereignty except in extreme circumstances such as when a nation engages in genocide against its own people. What is important here is that no nation's law supersedes that of another's, though nations can use economic and cultural enticements or punishments to try to affect change—or in extreme cases go to war. Relating this abstract discussion to IBCs, there is, on the one hand, an increasing trend toward higher education institutions transcending national boundaries, while, on the other hand, nations still have the authority to determine the rules and regulations within their own boundaries. Some nations may have complex layers of governments, such as in India, the United Arab Emirates, and the United States, where both national and state governments have some responsibility over education. When considering the impact of national sovereignty, one must understand the conditions in both the exporting and importing nations.

Exporting Governments. As stated elsewhere, the three largest exporters of higher education are Australia, the United Kingdom, and the United States. There is no evidence to suggest that such expansions are part of an official government effort. In each of these nations, the decision to establish a presence outside of the country remains with the institution. Suffice it to say that none of the countries expressly forbid such expansions, but they do generally disallow the use of government funding to support such

82   Multinational Colleges and Universities

endeavors (see, e.g., Lane, Kinser, and Knox 2009, for a discussion of state regulations of cross-border endeavors in the United States).

In Australia and the United Kingdom, there is evidence to suggest that government policies regarding government support of higher education may have indirectly encouraged the development of IBCs. For example, Mazzarol and Hosie (1997) argue that the broad-based expansion of Australian universities into foreign countries has been linked back to the Australian government's decision in 1985–1986 to allow their institutions to admit full-fee-paying foreign students. This alternative revenue stream helped offset declining government support (Mazzarol and Hosie 1997). Moreover, our own interviews with those responsible for opening IBCs of UK branches revealed that part of the motivation to expand was linked to government-imposed limits on the number of enrollment placements available to foreign students on the home campus. Opening branch campuses in another country allowed those institutions to set their own enrollment targets, at times operating larger academic programs abroad than on the home campus.

Importing Governments. Host countries appear to have a number of reasons for allowing the presence of foreign education providers, representing an interrelated set of political, economic, cultural, and pedagogical interest (Fegan and Field 2009). In particular, countries are interested in increasing local access to higher education, improving the domestic education sector providing academic programs and pedagogical practices not otherwise available in the host country, and helping improve the international reputation of the host country (Lane 2010; Lee 2003; McBurnie and Ziguras 2007; Wildavsky 2010). Some importing nations are particularly interested in attracting prestigious institutions or institutions from well-respected higher education systems in order to help improve the country's international reputation (Lane 2011).

Educational Hubs. A stated goal of many importing nations is the desire to become an *educational hub*. An educational hub is a designated region intended to attract foreign investment, retain local students, build a regional reputation by providing access to high-quality education and training for both international and domestic students, and create a knowledge-based economy. An education hub can include different combinations of domestic/international institutions, branch campuses, and foreign partnerships within the designated region. To date, the term appears to be primarily a rhetorical tool used to attract attention and drive the development of governmental policy. Indeed, the desire of many nations to become an educational hub has directly influenced the development of policy related to IBCs as such entities are often viewed as a means for transforming a nation into an educational hub. (Descriptions of many actual and planned educational hubs can be found at www.globalhighered.org.)

Hubs may differ substantially in terms of their goals, activities, and sponsors. Three basic hub categories suggested by Knight (2010), for example, reflect a progression of mission from serving as a center for international student recruitment, to a training center for the development of a skilled domestic workforce, to an innovation center that creates a critical mass of expertise for a knowledge-based economy.

Nations expressing an interest in becoming an educational hub are mostly scattered throughout Asia and the Middle East. And, in some nations, there are multiple hub-related strategies at play. For example, in the United Arab Emirates, at least three of the seven emirates have expressed separate intentions of becoming educational hubs. In South Korea, two different initiatives have been launched to create an education hub, one led by public actors and the other by private investors.

There are two general implementation strategies associated with the development of educational hubs (Kinser and Lane 2010). The first strategy usually focuses on developing the nation as an educational hub, and there is little concern about where IBCs or other educational institutions might be located. Thus, IBCs might be spread across a wide geographic area, not within close proximity to each other. This is referred to as an archipelago hub. The second strategy is represented by the acropolis hub, where there is a purposeful decision that institutions are to be located in very close proximity to each other, thus creating a focused site for the hub.

It is important to recognize that these two implementation strategies are not mutually exclusive. Countries can pursue an archipelago hub at the same time they designate certain areas for an acropolis hub. Malaysia is a good example here, which has several IBCs established near the capital city and in Malaysian Borneo, as well as two acropolis hubs: one in Kuala Lumpur, and the second on the country's border with Singapore. Nevertheless, the current environment suggests a growing influence of acropolis strategies globally. Countries perceive a distinct competitive advantage in recruiting IBCs to their shores through the concentrated and synchronous development of multiple campuses combined with an accommodating regulatory environment.

Archipelagoes. In the archipelago model, IBCs do not all operate in one location. For example, in China, South Africa, and Vietnam there are no special locations that the government has designated for new or existing IBCs. Like individual islands distributed across a stretch of ocean, IBCs are spread throughout the country. In such models, IBCs tend to operate in greater isolation from each other and are generally more integrated into the local higher education sector, rather than as a separate subsector. This integration means that regulation of archipelago IBCs is often conducted as if the institutions are domestic private-sector institutions, and individual branch campuses are seen as broadening and extending the host country's educational capacity, though IBCs in archipelago environments may be able to avail themselves of favorable policy incentives not available to their domestic counterparts, such as streamlined approval processes, flexibility in curricular requirements, and financial incentives. The government also

84 MULTINATIONAL COLLEGES AND UNIVERSITIES

provides rhetorical support for increasing foreign educational investments in the country by developing long-range plans that emphasize the economic development benefits of IBCs.

Acropolises. In an acropolis hub, several IBCs are located in very close proximity to each other, often within walking distance. Generally, there are shared physical spaces and some level of coordination among the institutions (sometimes such coordination is facilitated, and in other cases it emerges naturally from institutional proximity). Well-known acropolis hubs include Qatar Education City and Dubai International Academic City; lesser-known locations include Incheon in South Korea and Iskandar in Malaysia. The creation of such locations can serve to isolate IBCs from the rest of the local education sector. And how the hub is created can impact the operations of the IBCs. For example, in Qatar Education City, each IBC is selected by the Qatar Foundation and allowed to offer only certain degree programs. This regulation on the number of institutions and programs reduces competition and increases coordination. However, in Dubai International Academic City, there are a large number of institutions, many of which offer the same academic programs; thus, there tends to be more interinstitutional competition among those IBCs.

Conclusion

The policy context for IBC development is still in flux. But we can draw a few conclusions from current patterns. First, the influence of globalization has weakened barriers to cross-border higher education and has encouraged the exploration of international markets for and suppliers of educational services. Second, despite growing numbers of multinational colleges and universities, the national regulatory model remains robust, and countries have continued to assert their authority over any education that occurs within their domestic borders. Third, the competitive landscape is changing, and countries that wish to encourage IBC development are finding value in adjusting regulatory burdens and providing other inducements to attract high-quality providers. And, finally, outside of quality assurance activity, policies and regulations governing IBC development are provided by the host country to serve a domestic educational and economic agenda. In sum, the policy environment has become more accommodating of the multinational college and university, but a global standard has yet to emerge.

Note

1. Information from the US BEA is available at www.bea.gov/inter national/bp_web/simple.cfm?anon=71&table_id=22&area_id=3 and was accessed on February 28, 2011. Information from Australia's Department of Foreign Affairs and Trade was accessed on February 28, 2011 from www.dfat.gov.au/publications/tgs/partners-top10–2009.pdf.

References

Fegan, J., and M. H. Field. (eds.). 2009. *Education Across Borders: Politics, Policy and Legislative action.* New York: Springer.

Held, D., A. McGrew, D. Goldblatt, and J. Perraton. 1999. *Global Transformations: Politics, Economics, and Culture.* Stanford, CA: Stanford University Press.

Kinser, K., and J. E. Lane. 2010. "Educational Hubs: Archipelagos & Acropolises." *International Higher Education* 59: 18–19.

Knight, J. 2010. "Higher Education Crossing Borders: Programs and Providers on the Move." In *Higher Education in a Global Society,* edited by D. B. Johnstone, M.B. d'Ambrosio and P.J. Yakoboski, Cheltenham, UK: Edward Elgar Publishing.

Lane, J. E. 2010. *Higher Education, Free Zones, and Quality Assurance in Dubai.* Policy Paper. Dubai School of Government: Dubai.

Lane, J. E. 2011. "Importing Private Higher Education: International Branch Campuses." *Journal of Comparative Policy Analysis* 13 (4): 367–381.

Lane, J. E., K. Kinser, and D. Knox. 2009. "The Effects of Interstate Regulations on Cross-Border Public Higher Education." *Institute for Higher Education Governance and Law Policy Paper Series.* www.law.uh.edu/ihelg/series.html.

Lee, M. 2003. "International Linkages in Malaysian Private Higher Education." *International Higher Education* 53: 11.

Mazzarol, T., and P. Hosie. 1997. "Long Distance Teaching: The Impact of Offshore Programs and Information Technology on Academic Work." *Australian Universities' Review* 40(1): 20–24.

McBurnie, G., and C. Ziguras. 2007. *Transnational Education: Issue and Trends in Offshore Higher Education.* New York: Routledge.

MTI. 2004. *Growing Our Economy.* Ministry of Trade and Industry, Singapore Government, http://app.mti.gov.sg/data/pages/507/doc/DSE_recommend.pdf. Accessed January 15, 2011.

Nye, J. (2005). *Soft Power and Higher Education.* Paper for the EDUCAUSE Forum for the Future of Higher Education. Accessed February 28, 2011 www.bea.gov/international/bp_web/simple.cfm?anon=71&table_id=22&area_id=3.

Wildavsky, B. 2010. *The Great Brain Race: How Global Universities Are Reshaping the World.* Oxford, UK: Princeton University Press.

JASON E. LANE is an Assistant Professor, Senior Researcher at the Institute for Global Education Policy Studies, and Senior Fellow at the Rockefeller Institute of Government, State University of New York, Albany. He co-leads the Cross-Border Education Research Team (www.globalhighered.org).

KEVIN KINSER is an Associate Professor, Senior Researcher at the Institute for Global Education Policy Studies, State University of New York, Albany. He co-leads the Cross-Border Education Research Team (www.globalhighered.org).

This chapter provides an annotated bibliography of resources pertaining to IBCs.

Selected Resources and Bibliography

Cross-Border Education Research Team (C-BERT)

This collection of references has been selected to represent the breadth of emerging scholarship on cross-border higher education and is intended to provide further resources on a range of concerns surrounding cross-border higher education. Each section includes abstracts of key books, book chapters, and journal articles. Abstracts appear once under the most pertinent subject heading.

General

Altbach, P. G. "Why Branch Campuses May Be Unsustainable." *International Higher Education* 58 (2010): 2–3.
From 2006 to 2009 branch campuses increased by 43 percent, suggesting a strong immediate future for branches, although the longer term is more uncertain. Few branches are full campuses; most are small and offer specialized subjects such as business and information technology in order to take advantage of the market. Branches do not have the same infrastructure as home campuses, and they are unable to ensure a strong, present professoriate; thus, many courses are taught in intensive modules. Branches attempt to replicate home campus selectivity and quality, but this can be problematic depending on the home campus's reputation. A future risk to branch campuses is the unclear pace of host countries' expansion of local higher education.

Becker, R. F. J. *International Branch Campuses: Markets and Strategies.* London: Observatory on Borderless Higher Education, 2009.
This report updates OBHE's 2006 study of international branch campuses (IBCs). IBCs have increased by 43 percent since 2006, with US institutions dominant. IBCs usually originate from developed countries and operate in developing countries, but they are increasingly being established by developing countries in other developing countries. Increasing competition

88 MULTINATIONAL COLLEGES AND UNIVERSITIES

and several IBC closures reinforce the need for market research and strategic planning. With planning, home institutions can boost revenue through increased enrollment, while host countries can add to infrastructure and retain students to counter brain drain. IBC expansion is expected to continue, but with rapid growth, new challenges for home institutions, host countries, and students will emerge.

Chapman, D. W., and R. Sakamoto, eds. *Cross-Border Partnerships in Higher Education: Strategies and Issues.* **New York: Routledge, 2010.**

This book addresses the forms and challenges of higher education institutional partnerships across borders. Included is an overview of the state of cross-border higher education partnerships and a framework for their analysis. Differences in partnerships and how they relate to differences in institutional purposes are discussed. Noninstructional partnerships are covered, including research partnerships, faculty development initiatives, and quality assurance. The book also addresses the contributions of cross-border partnerships to the fields of nursing, business, and agriculture, as well as to community, national, and regional development.

Croom, P. "Motivations and Aspirations for International Branch Campuses." In *Cross Border Collaborations in Higher Education: Strategies and Issues,* **edited by D. W. Chapman and R. Sakamoto, 45–66. New York: Routledge, 2010.**

Croom analyzes the role of partners in international branch campuses. The author compares the partnership models of Japanese branch campuses during the 1980s and current branch campuses in Qatar and Dubai. Partnership relationships bear on a number of branch campus concerns, including regulation, financing, and operational and academic flexibility. Often, partners are motivated by an eagerness to announce a branch campus opening and do not engage in sufficient analysis of the partnership opportunity.

Fegan, J., and M. H. Field, eds. *Education Across Borders: Politics, Policy and Legislative Action.* **New York: Springer, 2009.**

This edited volume explores cross-border education from the political and policy perspective of the host country. While much of the focus on cross-border education has been on the United States and on capacity and capability issues, there has been less focus on the education process itself. Using case studies of Australia, Latin America, China, Ireland, Portugal, South Africa, and the United Kingdom, the book explores issues such as the knowledge economy, institutional and student mobility, language, teacher/faculty migration, impact on national education systems, articulation between secondary and higher education, and e-learning. Taken together, the cases illustrate how host-country environments are inseparable from their political, economic, cultural, and pedagogical particularities.

NEW DIRECTIONS FOR HIGHER EDUCATION • DOI:10.1002/he

Garrett, R. *International Branch Campuses: Scale and Significance.* London: Observatory on Borderless Higher Education, 2002.

This report offers an assessment of international branch campuses at the beginning of their growth. In 2002, only eighteen branch campuses were in operation, with another six scheduled to open. However, the reliability of the data is questionable, as no governments collected systematic data and there was variation in defining branch campuses.

IBCs are a continuation of long-standing efforts to recruit international students. Most branches are built on existing partnerships or alliances. Partnerships began as an exporting strategy for foreign institutions, but many ran into quality control issues. Branch campuses offer firmer corporate control, higher local profile, and an innovative way to stand out from competitors.

Green, M. F., P. D. Eckel, L. Calderon, and D. T. Luu. *Venturing Abroad: Delivering US Degrees through Overseas Branch Campuses and Programs.* Washington, DC: American Council on Education, 2007.

This report explores US overseas campuses, specifically, the extent of activity, motivations for establishing offshore programs, and the challenges that institutional leaders face in establishing branch campuses. Institutions pursue cross-border education because of push factors relating to institutional goals as well as the pull of emerging opportunities overseas. Cross-border education takes multiple forms, ranging from a minimal presence to full-fledged campuses. Branch campuses are offshored from public, private not-for-profit, and for-profit institutions. Current hot spots for offshoring education are China, Singapore, and India. The report recommends that leaders should consider their mission and strategy and decide whether institutional internationalization needs to include the opening of branch campuses.

Green, M. F., K. Kinser, and P. D. Eckel. *On the Ground Overseas: US Degree Programs and Branch Campuses Abroad.* Washington, DC: American Council on Education, 2008.

This report addresses opportunities and challenges faced by US institutions operating overseas branch campuses. Ten US institutions offering degrees abroad to non-US students are profiled. Four major themes are addressed: origins and drivers of programs; program creation; general advice for institutional leaders; and arguments or warnings about overseas degree programs. This report should be of special interest to organizational leaders in higher education who are considering or are in the process of creating overseas programs.

Kinser, K., and J. E. Lane. "Educational Hubs: Archipelagos & Acropolises." *International Higher Education* 59 (2010): 18–19.

Many developing nations, particularly in the Middle East and Southeast Asia, are pursuing strategies designed to situate their country as an "educational hub." However, while the term is often used, its usage is often ambiguous and/or confusing. The authors examine five major assumptions in the emerging discourse about hubs and then disentangle fact from fiction.

90 MULTINATIONAL COLLEGES AND UNIVERSITIES

Kinser, K., D. C. Levy, J. C. Silas Casillas, A. Bernasconi, S. Slantcheva-Durst, W. Otieno, et al. "The Global Growth of Private Higher Education." *ASHE Higher Education Report* 36 no.3 (2010): 63–76. San Francisco: Jossey-Bass.

The book examines the development of private higher education around the world, drawing on case studies of Bulgaria, Chile, Dubai, Mexico, Kenya, Thailand, and the United States. Two chapters in particular warrant examination by those interested in cross-border higher education. The chapter "Private Higher Education in Dubai: Growing Local versus Importing Local Campuses" provides an overview of the largest importer of international branch campuses and discusses related public policy issues. The other chapter, "The Private Nature of Cross-Border Education," reviews global trends related to international branch campuses and their private nature.

Knight, J. "Cross-border Education: An Analytical Framework for Program and Provider Mobility." In *Higher Education: Handbook of Theory and Research*, edited by J. C. Smart, Vol. XX1, 345–395. Dordecht, Netherlands: Springer, 2006.

This article outlines an analytical framework for cross-border education. Included is a discussion of the relationship between cross-border ventures and current trends in globalization and internationalization. An analysis of the rationales for cross-border ventures and their impacts is included, along with a global survey of the current status of cross-border ventures by region. A typology of cross-border education categorizes ventures according to type of provider (recognized higher education institutions [HEIs], commercial HEIs, etc.), mode of program mobility (franchise, twinning, joint degree, etc.), and mode of provider mobility (branch campus, teaching site, affiliation, etc.).

Lane, J. E. "Importing Private Higher Education: International Branch Campuses." *Journal of Comparative Policy Analysis*, 13, no.4 (2011): 367–81.

This article applies a typology of private higher education to the case of cross-border higher education. Using document analysis, interviews with campus administrators, and secondary data, Lane describes the development of cross-border higher education in Dubai and Malaysia and analyzes its fit with Levy's typology, which categorizes private higher education as offering something superior to what is available in the local higher education market (e.g., institutional prestige), something different (e.g., access to different student populations or different pedagogical models), or something more (e.g., absorbing excess demand). Cross-border education in Dubai and Malaysia is found to serve all of these functions to varying degrees.

Lane, J. E., M. C. Brown, and M. A. Pearcey. "Transnational Campuses: Obstacles and Opportunities for Institutional Research in the

Global Education Market." In "Unique Campus Contexts: Insights for Research and Assessment", edited by J. E. Lane and M. C. Brown. *New Directions for Institutional Research* 124: 49–62. San Francisco: Jossey-Bass, 2005.

The chapter focuses on a practitioner audience and outlines some of the major issues associated with creating an IBC: assessing foreign market capacity, recognition and transferability of credentials, accountability and quality assurance, and the impact of the General Agreement on Trade in Services (GATS). Each section provides an introduction to the topic and then presents a series of questions for decision makers to consider prior to opening an IBC.

Lane, J. E., and K. Kinser. "The Private Nature of Cross-Border Higher Education." *International Higher Education* 53 (2008): 11.

The article focuses on public colleges and universities that open an IBC. It argues that though the home campus may be classified as public by the home government, the IBC will almost always exist as part of the private sector in the host government. Indeed, most IBCs are tuition-dependent operations, receiving little or no funding from the home or host governments. As such, while the IBC may benefit from the administrative infrastructure or reputation of the home campus, the IBC will have to learn to adapt to its local environmental conditions. The authors introduce the concept of "nonendemic" academics as a way to describe this phenomenon.

Lane, J. E. and K. Kinser. "Reconsidering Privatization in Cross-Border Engagements: The Sometimes Public Nature of Private Activity." *Higher Education Policy* 24 (2011): 255–73. Selected for the 2010 International Association of Universities – Palgrave Prize in Higher Education Policy Research.

This article examines how cross-border higher education challenges traditional notions of privatization, which are exclusively based on the perspective of the home government/campus. However, the authors argue that in cross-border engagements, it is important to examine an activity from the perspective of both the home and host governments. Using examples from Qatar and Sarawak, Malaysia, the authors demonstrate how governments may use IBCs to fulfill traditionally public service missions even though the home government/campus may view the same activity as private in nature.

McBurnie, G., and C. Ziguras. *Transnational Education: Issues and Trends in Offshore Higher Education.* New York: Routledge, 2007.

This book views transnational education from economic, political, cultural, technological, governmental, and university perspectives. Off-shoring campuses and host countries can set up cross-border operations through distance, partner-supported, or branch campus modes, with each mode having unique benefits and detriments. Failure can potentially drain home-campus resources, while success can enhance research opportunities and increase revenue. Host countries are concerned about cultural imperialism and ensuring high-quality academic programs. By minimizing cultural imperialism and ensuring high academic quality, host countries might gain prestige in their regions, attract and retain international and domestic students, and create a knowledge-based economy. Success for all actors relies on strong, understood, and mutually agreed upon contracts, procedures, and policies.

Naidoo, J. "Transnational Higher Education: A Stock Taking of Current Activity." *Journal of Studies in International Education* 13, no.3 (2009): 310–30.

Naidoo analyzes secondary data to assess the growth of transnational higher education. Transnational higher education has become a form of "academic trade." Franchising, twinning degrees, program articulations, branch campuses, virtual/distance learning, and corporate programs are listed as ways that transnational higher education is currently provided. It is noted that there is a concentration in eastern Europe, the Middle East, South America, and the Asian-Pacific. Australia exports more programs than any other country, but most cross-border tertiary institutions that are wholly owned emanate from the United States, followed closely by Britain. The article notes that US for-profit higher education institutions dominate the cross-border higher education landscape.

Naidoo, V. "Transnational Higher Education: Why It Happens and Who Benefits?" *International Higher Education* 58 (2010): 6–7.

Four rationales explain recent growth in transnational higher education. The Mutual Understanding perspective highlights the academic, cultural, social, and political bases for engaging in transnational programs. The Skilled Migration rationale emphasizes efforts to draw international students to source countries in order to increase the country's skilled labor. Transnational programs feed students to a source country through transfer between branch and home campuses. Revenue Generation describes income seeking as a motivation for transnational programs. Capacity Building views transnational education as a means of filling demand for higher education in receiving countries. Despite common perceptions that the benefits of transnational education accrue primarily to source countries, there are wide-ranging impacts that accrue to both receivers and senders.

Verbik, L., and C. Merkley. *The International Branch Campus—Models and Trends*. London: Observatory on Borderless Higher Education, 2006.

This report describes three models of branch campuses. Model A is a branch fully funded by the institution; this is the least common of the three models. In Model B, branches are externally funded by governments or private sources. Model C uses facilities provided by the host government; this model is found most often in economically advanced countries in the Persian Gulf. Institutions appear increasingly reluctant to absorb the entire cost of establishing a branch campus (Model A), leading to an increase in Models B and C.

Arab Gulf

Bashshur, M. "Observations from the Edge of the Deluge: Are We Going Too Far, Too Fast in Our Educational Transformation in the Arab Gulf?" In *Trajectories of Education in the Arab World: Legacies and Challenges*, edited by O. Abi-Mershed, 247–72. New York: Routledge, 2010.

This book chapter reflects on recent education reforms in the Arab Gulf region at the primary, secondary, and tertiary levels. While Qatar's Education City attracts high-profile, world-class institutions, only 4.4 percent of Qatari students are enrolled in foreign branches. The lack of Qatari students diminishes the impact of Education City on Qatari education. Dubai has established a similar education free trade zone, while Saudi Arabia has begun incorporating elements of Western-style education. Bashshur suggests that Arab higher education would better benefit from mutual collaboration and a sharing of expertise and resources than from importing foreign branch campuses, which tend to operate in isolation with limited enrollment of local students.

Krieger, Z. "Academic Building Boom Transforms the Persian Gulf." *Education Digest* 74, no.1 (2008): 4–10.

Krieger examines the strategies of Qatar, Abu Dhabi, and Dubai in importing higher education. Qatar provides funding and autonomy to selected American universities to establish branches and pays Qatari students' tuitions, with the objective of training Qatari citizens. Dubai's Knowledge Village is oriented toward generating profit since the emirate lacks Qatar's oil wealth. Its international branches can return their profits to their home countries. Abu Dhabi is the wealthiest emirate and has successfully attracted high-profile institutions from France and the United States. Importation of higher education has been criticized as serving "a narrow segment of society." It is suggested that foreign branches may weaken students' links to the society in which they were raised.

Wilkins, S. "Higher Education in the United Arab Emirates: An Analysis of the Outcomes of Significant Increases in Supply and Competition." *Journal of Higher Education Policy and Management* 32, no.4 (2010): 389–400.

This study analyzes the impacts of the UAE's saturated higher education market on student recruitment, student experiences, quality, and institutional strategies. Findings indicate that institutions face difficulty differentiating themselves in a crowded marketplace. Quality is also a concern, as the highest-quality students choose to study abroad or to attend

94 MULTINATIONAL COLLEGES AND UNIVERSITIES

public universities. Student shortages prompt some institutions to lower admission standards, causing concerns about institutional prestige. Student retention concerns pressure faculty to satisfy student demands, leading to grade inflation and diminished quality. Research capacity is inhibited in the humanities and social sciences by conservative political environments. Wilkins recommends that institutions recruit students from outside the UAE, operate more like businesses to differentiate themselves, and focus on customer satisfaction.

Asia

Chan, D., and P. T. Ng. "Developing Transnational Higher Edu-cation: Comparing the Approaches of Hong Kong and Singapore." *International Journal of Educational Reform* **17, no. 3 (2008): 291–307.**
This article compares the approaches of Hong Kong and Singapore in attracting transnational education providers by examining the development of transnational education along five dimensions: goals, business approach, culture, process, and resources. The authors find that while Hong Kong and Singapore share a common goal of becoming a regional education hub, they vary in the other dimensions. Hong Kong has a liberal free market approach with institutions operating relatively independently from government and without government resources. In contrast, Singapore has a detailed strategy for transnational education development with close regulation of foreign universities and the offer of financial incentives to attract top foreign universities.

Huang, F. "Internationalization of Higher Education in the Developing and Emerging Countries: A Focus on Transnational Higher Education in Asia." *Journal of Studies in International Education* **11, no. 3/4 (2007): 421–32.**
This article categorizes Asian transnational higher education according to three types: Import-Oriented, Import & Export, and Transitional. Vietnam and Indonesia import education, while Singapore and Hong Kong both import and export higher education. China and Japan are transitional countries that predominantly import foreign higher education but also export higher education to a small degree. A variety of national policies and strategies exist in Asia, ranging from government regulated to market driven. Huang argues that Asia is the most important and active region for transnational higher education. As transnational higher education grows and is increasingly supported, it is forming an integral component of national higher education in many Asian countries.

Lane, J. E. "Joint Ventures in Cross-Border Higher Education: International Branch Campuses in Malaysia." In *Cross Border Collaborations in Higher Education: Partnerships Beyond the Classroom,* **edited by D. W. Chapman and R. Sakamoto, 67–90. New York: Routledge, 2010.**

This chapter explains the three primary types of organizational structures that are used when creating an IBC: joint venture, strategic alliance, and wholly owned subsidiary. The chapter then examines the types of governance arrangements that might be used in the creation of a joint venture between a foreign education provider and a local development firm. There is a specific focus on how governance structures can impact the flow of information between the campus and the potential negative repercussions of when such structures limit the interaction between the partners. The chapter uses examples from two Australian universities that established IBCs in Malaysia in the 1990s.

Lee, M. "International Linkages in Malaysian Private Higher Education." *International Higher Education*, 30 (2003): 17–9.

This article outlines the types of international linkages in Malaysian private higher education. Program curricula, syllabi, and exams are often created by foreign institutions, with local providers teaching and administering examinations. Such programs often lead to a credential awarded by the foreign institution. Twinning programs are similarly structured, with foreign institutions playing an active role in monitoring and ensuring quality. Students who complete the Malaysian program are guaranteed transfer admission to the foreign institution. Under credit transfer arrangements, students can earn credits at a private institution in Malaysia and then transfer those credits to an institution abroad if admitted. Distance education and foreign branch campuses are also present.

McBurnie, G. "Transnational Education, Quality, and the Public Good: Case Studies from South-East Asia." In *Globalization and the Market in Higher Education: Quality, Accreditation, and Qualifications*, edited by S. Uvalić-Trumbić, 159–70. Paris: UNESCO, 2002.

McBurnie examines public benefits of transnational education in East Asia, including contributions to local economies. Transnational education has contributed to educational capacity in East Asia by increasing student enrollments. Legislative instruments are in place to prevent public funds from being used for transnational education. In Malaysia, students' rights are protected through legislation to prevent substandard courses. Information on courses is provided to transnational educators. To ensure optimum quality, transnational course offerings undergo accreditation in home countries before they are offered in the importing country. McBurnie notes that the state has a powerful role in ensuring quality.

Mok, K. H., and X. Xu. "When China Opens to the World: A Study of Transnational Higher Education in Zhejiang, China." *Asia Pacific Education Review* 9, no. 4 (2008): 393–408.

China's economic growth has engendered rapid advancements in science and information technology. To meet the challenges of the growing knowledge-based economy, the Chinese government has begun to allow overseas universities to offer educational programs. This article examines the policy

96   MULTINATIONAL COLLEGES AND UNIVERSITIES

context of allowing transnational higher education in China, with special reference to how foreign programs would affect Chinese higher education.

Olds, K. "Global Assemblage: Singapore, Foreign Universities, and the Construction of a 'Global Education Hub'." *World Development* 35, no. 6 (2007): 959–75.

The need for enhanced services and a better-educated and more skilled citizenry has led to the elevation of principles of lifelong learning, creativity, innovation, entrepreneurship, and critical thinking in Singapore. To transform Singapore into the "Boston of the East," foreign higher education institutions have been viewed as playing a fundamental role in restructuring the economy. Utilizing foreign institutions will assist Singapore in creating a knowledge hub in which a confluence of people and ideas act as an incubator for innovation.

Wilmoth, D. "RMIT Vietnam and Vietnam's Development: Risk and Responsibility." *Journal of Studies in International Education* 8, no. 2 (2004): 186–206.

To bridge the gap between demand and supply, Vietnam has opened the country to foreign providers, with the Royal Melbourne Institute of Technology (RMIT) International University Vietnam becoming the first foreign institution to offer higher education in Vietnam. RMIT relies on fees, so its programs must be effective and affordable. Operating a campus near Ho Chi Minh City, RMIT is under pressure to demonstrate that foreign higher education is sustainable. To establish itself socially and culturally, RMIT has established local projects, provided scholarships, and assisted local universities in capacity building.

Development Perspectives

Lien, D. "Economic Analysis of Transnational Education." *Education Economics* 16, no. 2 (2008): 149–66.

Lien examines the impact of foreign branch campuses on the economic welfare of developing countries. Lower-ranked foreign branch campuses have greater value to a developing country than highly ranked institutions because graduates from branches of highly ranked institutions have opportunities to emigrate for higher incomes, thereby increasing brain drain. Graduates from lower-ranked branch campuses may not command high salaries through emigration, and thus limit brain drain and enhance the social welfare of the home country.

Middlehurst, R., and S. Woodfield. *The Role of Transnational, Private, and For-Profit Provision in Meeting Global Demand for Tertiary Education: Mapping, Regulation and Impact.* **Vancouver: Commonwealth of Learning/ Paris: UNESCO, 2004.**

This report maps transnational, private, and for-profit tertiary education in Jamaica, Bangladesh, Malaysia, and Bulgaria. Demand for tertiary education is increasing in all sample countries. Increased demand often results from increasing per capita income, improvements in primary and secondary education, and inflexible supply from the public system. Countries had similar goals for widening tertiary education, including increasing access, increasing economic relevance of education, improving quality, enhancing science and technology, and stimulating national identity. Despite similarities, there were subtle differences between countries.

OECD. *Cross-Border Tertiary Education: A Way towards Capacity Development*. Paris: Author, 2007.

This book analyzes cross-border higher education's potential to contribute to host countries' development. Jane Knight examines cross-border higher education's growth and complexity, terminology, diversity of providers, program and institutional typologies, rationales and impact, and emerging issues and challenges. Stephan Vincent-Lancrin discusses the reasons for building higher education capacity, incorporation of cross-border education into development strategy, potential contributions of capacity building to higher education, and the complementarity of trade and development assistance in cross-border higher education. Richard Hopper examines the challenge of building capacity in quality assurance, including quality assurance complexities and ideal versus manageable systems. Massimo Geloso-Grosso focuses on developing capacity in tertiary education through trade liberalization, investment, regulation and remedial policies, higher education services, and the GATS.

Vincent-Lancrin, S. *Building Capacity through Cross-Border Tertiary Education*. London: Observatory on Borderless Higher Education, 2005.

The use of education as a capacity-building and economic development tool is a recent phenomenon with little data regarding its effectiveness. In some cases, partnering with foreign institutions offers an opportunity for joint programs or degrees. Other examples of tertiary cross-border education involve distance learning. All forms are currently delivered under a variety of contractual arrangements. The report contains guidelines to be used by countries seeking to benefit from cross-border education.

Management

Dunworth, K. "Ideas and Realities: Investigating Good Practice in the Management of Transnational English Language Programmes for the Higher Education Sector." *Quality in Higher Education* 14, no. 2 (2008): 95–107.

This study investigates the management of transnational English language teaching programs to identify best practices and factors influencing their implementation. Interviews and document analysis were conducted for three sites in Indonesia and Mauritius. Findings indicate that best practices include: both partners' undertaking due diligence and including all stakeholders; both partners' familiarizing themselves with the cultural and

98   MULTINATIONAL COLLEGES AND UNIVERSITIES

educational context of the host country; and programs' receiving adequate resources to maintain program quality.

Edwards, R., and J. Edwards. "Internationalisation of Education: A Business Perspective." *Australian Journal of Education* **45, no. 1 (2001): 76–89.**

This article analyzes education export from four theoretical perspectives. Internationalization theory explains higher education export as more efficient than moving large numbers of international students across borders. Dunning's eclectic paradigm justifies higher education export on the basis that exporting institutions have advantages of ownership, internationalization, and location. The Uppsala model views higher education export as an incremental process. Vernon's product life cycle model is found to be a poor fit for higher education, but may apply to developing countries that venture into education export. Comparisons are made between exporting education institutions and multinational corporations.

Feast, V., and T. Bretag. "Responding to Crises in Transnational Education: New Challenges for Higher Education." *Higher Education Research and Development* **24, no. 1 (2005): 63–78.**

Feast and Bretag investigate how the SARS epidemic impacted home campus staff of an Australian institution with an Asian transnational program. Two focus groups were conducted with academic and administrative staff. The article reports participants' perceptions of changes in work practices, health issues, personal matters, student needs, and miscellaneous issues as a result of the SARS epidemic that disrupted the university's normal delivery of its transnational program. Participants indicated increased workloads and stress levels, which were partly attributed to the lack of contingency planning in advance.

Hefferman, T., and D. Poole. "'Catch Me I'm Falling'": Key Facts in the Deterioration of Offshore Education Partnerships." *Journal of Higher Education Policy and Management* **26, no. 1 (2004): 75–90.**

Hefferman and Poole research the early interaction phase of Australian programs in Southeast Asia using ten case studies and interviews. The type of investment made during the early building phase is a crucial factor that can lead to success or failure. Findings were consistent with other studies in that the absence of trust, commitment, and effective communication led to deterioration of offshore education partnerships. The level of internal commitment by an Australian university, the identification of roles and responsibilities of the partners, the establishment of a non–win/win relationship, and the departure of key personnel were factors occurring during the early phase of offshore partnerships that later weakened the relationship.

Kim, E. H., and M. Zhu. "Universities as Firms: The Case of US Overseas Programs." In *American Universities in a Global Market,* **edited by C. T. Clotfelter 163–204. Chicago: University of Chicago Press, 2010.**

This study compares higher education institutions to firms using economic analysis. Organizational structure, objective function, stakeholder interests, and governance are considered. Higher education's accountability to multiple stakeholders and their institutional governance are found to be more complex than firms. There were differences in economic motives, demand, alternative choices, assets, and variable costs. Analysis of branch campuses from 1988 to 2008 concluded that US overseas branches were similar to firms engaging in foreign direct investment. US institutions seek countries with flexible legislation, a business friendly environment, and a large applicant pool. Branch campuses adapt tuition to local competitors to gain student enrollment. Firms behave similarly when investing in a foreign country.

McBurnie, G., and A. Pollock. "Decision Making for Offshore Activities: A Case Study on Monash University." In edited by D. Davis, A. Olsen, and A. Bohm. *Transnational Education Providers, Partners and Policy: Challenges for Australian Institutions Offshore.* Canberra: IDP Education Australia, 2000.

Using a case study of Monash University, this chapter describes how institutions make decisions about establishing overseas programs. Strategic, educational, and business components of decision making are explored. The strategic component is influenced by the university's teaching, research, and service functions. Country selection depends on the compatibility of educational philosophy with host country infrastructure. The educational component ensures that programs match the institution's academic goals. The business component involves assessing rewards and risks, which vary between centrally driven and departmentally based program proposals. Centrally driven proposals involving the entire university campus have high costs, and departmental proposals are less expensive. Market research is conducted to determine whether an offshore program is cost effective.

Vinen, D. G., and C. Selvarajah. "A Framework for Sustainability of an Offshore Education Program: A Systems Based Approach." *Journal of International Business and Economics* 8, no. 2 (2008): 160–69.

A case study of an Australian accounting program in Vietnam is used to explore factors contributing to the sustainability of cross-border education. Stakeholder theory is used to conceptualize cross-border educational enterprises as complex systems. Findings indicate five critical success factors common to all stakeholders: reputation of the Australian university, professional accreditation of the program, effective partnership between the universities, flexible program delivery, and student opportunities to study in Australia. The authors suggest a systematic approach for developing sustainable offshore programs: (1) program planning and development, (2) program accreditation, (3) program predelivery, (4) program delivery, and (5) program postdelivery. Activities to promote success are proposed for each stage.

Yiyun, J. "International Partnerships: A Game Theory Perspective." *New Directions for Higher Education*, no. 150 (2010): 43–54.

This chapter utilizes game theory to investigate how divergent partner motivations and outcome expectations create synergy and present

100 MULTINATIONAL COLLEGES AND UNIVERSITIES

implementation challenges in Sino-US cross border higher education. A case study of a partnership between a Chinese business school and an elite US institution is used. Findings indicate a high congruence of motivations between the two institutions, including enhancing brand influences, generating revenue, and providing faculty and student learning opportunities. However, once the program was established, outcome preferences diverged between the institutions, including the priority of brand influence versus enrollment size. Findings were consistent with the game theory framework and predictions.

Quality

Blackmur, D. "A Critical Analysis of the UNESCO/OECD Guidelines for Quality Provision of Cross-Border Higher Education." *Quality in Higher Education* 13, no. 2 (2007): 117–130.

This article criticizes elements of the 2003 UNESCO guidelines on practices and principles in transnational education, arguing that the guidelines have been developed without consideration of the potential negative and positive benefits associated with implementation. The author discusses several important implications and limitations of the guidelines.

Coleman, D. "Quality Assurance in Transnational Education." *Journal of Studies in International Education* 7, no. 4 (2003): 354–78.

This study investigates the consistency of delivery of academic content for a transnational academic program. A total of 88 student and staff interviews were conducted across two branch campuses—one in Jakarta, Indonesia, and another in Kuala Lumpur, Malaysia. Comparing interview data with university documents, Coleman finds that contrary to university mechanisms designed to ensure the sameness of academic programs, differences in teaching and testing exist. Study participants demonstrate no consensus regarding the relationship between the home campus and branch campus or the desired composition of the most effective teaching staff.

Edwards, J., G, Crosling, and R. Edwards. "Outsourcing University Degrees: Implications for Quality Control." *Journal of Higher Education Policy and Management* 32, no. 3 (2010): 303–15.

As educational institutions establish overseas programs, quality control becomes increasingly important. The authors apply transaction cost analysis to the issue of quality control. The report concludes that there is a risk when developing license arrangements and that universities should carefully monitor all contracts. The authors recommend that quality control systems should be implemented to assess the financial viability of overseas partners, that teaching and assessment standards be studied, and that all marketing material be examined for content and accuracy.

Knight, J. "Cross-Border Higher Education: Issues and Implications for Quality Assurance and Accreditation." In *Higher Education in the*

World 2007: Accreditation for Quality Assurance: What Is at Stake?, edited by Global University Network for Innovation, 134–46. New York: Palgrave Macmillan, 2007.

While cross-border education providers seek accreditation to ensure the legitimacy of their institutions and programs, distinguishing between genuine and illegitimate accreditation agencies is a challenge. In response, Knight proposes a registry of genuine accreditation agencies. For exporting countries, regulations help protect students and partner institutions from low quality, illegitimate providers. Regulations aid importing countries by ensuring growing access to higher education and lessening brain drain. Disadvantages include foreign institutions pulling out if profit margins are low and the restriction of cross-border education to those with an ability to pay.

Lane, J. E. *Higher Education, Free Zones, and Quality Assurance in Dubai*. Policy Paper. Dubai: Dubai School of Government, 2010.

In this policy brief, published by the Dubai School of Government, Professor Lane analyzes the role of international branch campuses in the development of Dubai's higher education sector, discusses major public policy issues, and explains the array of free zones used to import IBCs. His findings highlight that almost half of the emirate's higher education sector is comprised of foreign education providers, most of the academic programs are professional in nature, and that there are conflicting regulations from the federal and emirate governments concerning the operation of IBCs.

Lim, F.C.B. "Education Hub at a Crossroads: The Development of Quality Assurance as a Competitive Tool for Singapore's Private Tertiary Education." *Quality Assurance in Education* 17, no. 1 (2008): 79–94.

Lim investigates how national quality assurance schemes are understood and implemented at two private higher education institutions in Singapore, both offering franchised programs from overseas institutions. Twelve staff members were interviewed. Interviewees perceived effective measures of quality as those relating to education delivery practices, including student evaluations, examinations, and teacher observations. National quality frameworks relate to business practices and are not perceived as improving quality.

Lim, F.C.B. "Understanding Quality Assurance: A Cross Country Case Study." *Quality Assurance in Education* 16, no. 2 (2008): 126–40.

Lim investigates differences in perceptions of quality assurance between an Australian university and its offshore partner in Malaysia. Both partners viewed audits of the offshore program as superficial and not effective in enhancing quality. Interviewees were evenly divided on whether the university should be ultimately responsible for quality or if the responsibility should be shared. Agreement was found on existing quality measures and objectives, but perceptions varied on what it meant to provide programs that were "comparable" to the university's domestic courses. While interviewees at all levels in Malaysia were aware of quality assurance policies, Australian administrators were aware and faculty were not. Partners agreed that student assessment was the most effective quality assurance policy.

Rawazik, W., and M. Carroll. "Complexity in Quality Assurance in a Rapidly Growing Free Economic Environment: A UAE Case Study." *Quality in Higher Education* 15, no. 1 (2009): 79–83.

In response to higher education demand, the United Arab Emirates has increased higher education opportunities for Emiratis. Additionally, universities from the United States, United Kingdom, and Australia have established campuses to satisfy demand from UAE's expatriate population. The government has established the Knowledge and Human Development Authority (KHDA) to assure quality of branch campuses. KHDA's model focuses on ensuring equivalent quality between the branch and its home campus. The Universities Quality Assurance International Board (UQAIB) aids quality assurance by providing the KHDA with independent and international information. Besides the KHDA, the UAE has two other quality assurance bodies; differences between the quality assurance systems present a challenge of mutual recognition between them.

Stella, A. "Quality Assurance of Cross-Border Higher Education." *Quality in Higher Education* 12, no. 3 (2006): 257–76.

This article provides background on UNESCO-OECD's *Guidelines for Quality Provision in Cross-Border Higher Education*. The negotiations were informed by four views of cross-border higher education: the international view, the disadvantaged view, the trade promoter's view, and the view that cross-border education is a nonissue. UNESCO-OECD's cooperative quality assurance framework is necessary because of the increasing internationalization of higher education; cross-border higher education's value for developing countries; and the increased need to demonstrate legitimacy in response to rogue providers. The article concludes with the scope of the guidelines, sending and receiving country perspectives, discussion of good practices, and future directions.

Woodhouse, D. "The Quality of Transnational Education: A Provider View." *Quality in Higher Education* 12, no. 3 (2006): 277–81.

This article describes the Australian Universities Quality Assurance Agency's (AUQA) role in quality assurance for Australian transnational education. AUQA has experienced challenges in conducting onsite overseas audits, as they are expensive and burdensome. AUQA has responded by creating a framework of triggers that activate an onsite audit, rather than auditing all overseas programs. Additional challenges include host country perceptions of overseas audits as "quality assurance colonization"; lack of interaction with the host country's agencies; and AUQA's lack of jurisdiction over partner institutions. AUQA has sought to alleviate these issues by memoranda of cooperation with host country quality assurance agencies.

Students

Wilkins, S., and J. Huisman. "Student Recruitment at International Branch Campuses: Can They Compete in the Global Market?" *Journal of Studies in International Education* (published online December 6, 2010): 1–8.

To understand the student market facing international branch campuses, this study investigates the motivations of international students. Surveys of 160 international students in the United Kingdom identified factors influencing students' decisions to study overseas, factors contributing to institutional choice, and whether students would consider an IBC. A logit model was developed to predict the likelihood that a student would consider an international branch campus. The model accurately predicted 96.6 percent of the students who indicated they would not consider an international branch campus and 37.8 percent of students who indicated they would consider an international branch. Reputation and quality were significant in students' institutional selection, suggesting that the ability of IBCs to provide quality research and instruction may relate to their ability to enroll students.

Teaching and Learning

Debowski, S. "Across the Divide: Teaching a Transnational MBA in a Second Language." *Higher Education Research and Development* 24, no. 3 (2005): 265–80.

China represents a growing market for transnational programs, but many challenges exist for schools that seek to offer high-quality learning in a cost-effective manner. Bilingual programs are especially challenged to establish an effective teaching-learning environment when teaching involves the use of translators. Especially difficult is monitoring learning outcomes. This article identifies some ways in which teaching staff in bilingual programs can be supported.

Dunn, L., and M. Wallace, eds. *Teaching in Transnational Higher Education*. New York: Routledge, 2008.

This book presents wide-ranging perspectives on teaching in transnational education programs. Part I discusses key emerging issues facing transnational education, including actors' needs and motivations, power differentials between exporting and importing countries, and how these concerns relate to the delivery, content, and quality of transnational education. Part II addresses the tensions between Western-style education and the adaptation of teaching practice to local contexts. Part III explores how students experience transnational education, including how transnational students experience curricula that aim to impart values of internationalism, multiculturalism, and collaborative and independent learning. Part IV addresses risks that institutions face when engaging in transnational activity.

104   MULTINATIONAL COLLEGES AND UNIVERSITIES

Several case studies highlight difficulties faced by transnational programs. The final chapters present recommendations for improving transnational education for teachers, students, institutions, and others.

Gribble, K., and C. Ziguras. "Learning to Teach Offshore: Pre-departure Training for Lecturers in Transnational Programs." *Higher Education Research and Development* 22, no. 2 (2003): 205–16.

The authors investigate the training of offshore lecturers, its perceived relevance and usefulness, and views on the preferred types of preparation. Of the twenty offshore lecturers interviewed, none participated in predeparture training, although many participated in cross-cultural teaching and learning workshops. Lecturers valued informal mentoring with experienced offshore faculty because changing host-country conditions quickly make formal training obsolete; formal training is too generic; and experienced lecturers are viewed as more knowledgeable. Interviewees viewed onshore teaching of foreign students as adequate preparation for teaching abroad. Recommendations include providing information about general issues that lecturers routinely face, providing country-specific information relevant to offshore contexts, and developing systems to enhance informal support and sharing of information.

Hussin, V. "Supporting Off-Shore Students: A Preliminary Study." *Innovations in Education and Teaching International* 44, no. 4 (2007): 363–76.

Hussin investigates learning support services for Asian students in Australian transnational programs. Fifteen staff members from twelve Australian universities were surveyed about the programs available to transnational students. Eleven universities operated websites with general learning support information (study skills, academic grammar); seven institutions offered online materials (web tutorials, workshops); six institutions offered e-mail consultations; five institutions offered in-country programs; and four institutions provided support through CD-ROMs. Many services educated students on avoiding plagiarism. In-country programs and e-mail consultations were found to be the most effective forms of learning support, but they also have the heaviest staff workload, so they may not be sustainable on a wide-scale basis. A model for collaborative learning development for transnational students is proposed.

Kelly, M. E., and S. H. Tak. "Borderless Education and Teaching and Learning Cultures: The Case of Hong Kong." *Australian Universities' Review* 41, no. 1 (1998): 26–33.

This article challenges stereotypes of Asian learners' favoring rote memorization; relying on content rather than argument; being reluctant to challenge, discuss, or critique; and expecting the teacher to deliver "correct" answers. Research suggests that while Asian students engage in memorization, they do so to gain deeper understanding rather than as the end goal of education. Stereotypes of authoritarian Asian teachers are challenged when

NEW DIRECTIONS FOR HIGHER EDUCATION • DOI:10.1002/he

considering the mentoring relationships that occur outside class and the individualized instruction that Asian teachers provide. When teaching across cultural borders, it cannot be assumed that Asian students will adapt to Western teaching styles. Cultural borders must be considered alongside political, economic, and regulatory borders when designing and implementing cross-border higher education programs.

Rostron, M. "Liberal Arts Education in Qatar: Intercultural Perspectives." *Intercultural Education* 20, no. 3 (2009): 219–29.

This article explores tensions between the liberal arts perspective of Western higher education and the expectations of Qataris for transnational programs. Qatari education is historically rooted in religious instruction, oral tradition, memorization, and transmission of knowledge. Liberal arts values of education as dialogue, active learning, and critical thinking have exposed tensions as Western education institutions have opened programs in Qatar. Historical foundations of Qatari education and liberal arts education are described. The article describes Qatar's internal debate on the drawbacks and benefits of Western-style education in the country.

Ziguras, C. "Educational Technology in Transnational Higher Education in Southeast Asia: The Cultural Politics of Flexible Learning." *Educational Technology and Society* 4, no. 4 (2001): 8–18.

This article examines educational technology in transnational higher education in Southeast Asia. Although some technologies are appropriate for some countries, use of technology is not appropriate in nations in Southeast Asia, where instruction has traditionally been teacher-directed. Ziguras examines government policies on technology use in higher education in Singapore, Malaysia, and Vietnam, and reviews the experiences of five institutions that have offered higher education in those countries.

Trade and Regulation

Knight, J. *Higher Education Crossing Borders: A Guide to the Implications of the General Agreement on Trade in Services (GATS) for Cross-Border Education.* Vancouver: Commonwealth of Learning/Paris: UNESCO, 2006.

Knight examines transnational higher education and the General Agreement on Trade in Services (GATS), which aims to decrease trade restrictions. Under GATS, cross-border education can be categorized into four supply procedures, each with its own restrictions. "Cross-border supply" includes distance learning and virtual universities, with restrictions on educational material. "Consumption abroad" involves participation in study abroad programs, with limits on travel depending on area of study. "Commercial presence" refers to local branches, with regulations stipulating local partnership. "Presence of natural persons" is restricted by visa and entry limitations. Controversial elements of GATS are examined, including governmental provision

106   MULTINATIONAL COLLEGES AND UNIVERSITIES

of higher education, countries' abilities to regulate higher education within their borders, and quality assurance and accreditation.

McBurnie, G., and C. Ziguras. "Remaking the World in Our Own Image: Australia's Efforts to Liberalise Trade in Education Service." *Australian Journal of Education* 47, no. 3 (2003): 217–34.

This article details Australia's efforts to liberalize trade in education services during GATS negotiations. Australia has been active in promoting trade liberalization largely because of the country's interest in growing its education export industry. Many other countries associate Australia's international efforts with a market-driven orientation rather than one of educational quality. In response, Australia has increasingly focused on quality assurance and internationalization of curricula.

OECD. *Internationalisation and Trade in Higher Education: Opportunities and Challenges*. Paris: Author, 2004.

This book reviews cross-border education in North America, Europe, and the Asia-Pacific region. Discussion of the development of cross-border education and the rationales for each region are included. Emphasis is placed on relevant government policies regulating cross-border education and their impact on student access, cost, quality, and capacity building. An argument is made for greater policy coherence among governments and stakeholders.

Verbik, L., and L. Jokivirta. *National Regulatory Frameworks for Transnational Higher Education: Models and Trends, Part 1 & Part 2*. London: Observatory on Borderless Higher Education, 2005.

Part 1: Institutions' reluctance or inability to carry the costs and risks of establishing international campuses has led to an increase in collaborative provision. However, uncertain operating environments could potentially lead to institutions' decreased willingness to operate under a model that affords limited control over certain aspects of the operation.

Part 2: This report discusses concerns over regulation of transnational education. While some countries have developed regulations for foreign providers, many do not regulate transnational education. The move toward regulation appears driven by concerns over quality. Case studies of Malaysia, Japan, South Africa, and Greece are included. Also included is information on regulatory models used in the case study countries, as well as Belgium, Bulgaria, Cyprus, India, South Korea, and the United Arab Emirates.

Ziguras, C. "The Impact of the GATS on Transnational Tertiary Education: Comparing Experiences of New Zealand, Australia, Singapore, and Malaysia." *Australian Educational Researcher* 30, no. 3 (2003): 89–110.

The need for higher education in Malaysia has prompted the government to establish a regional education hub and the passage of the Private Higher Education Institution Act of 1996. The act allows for increases in private higher education and is regarded as important for Malaysian higher education. IBCs have improved the framework of Malaysian higher education and have significantly reduced the country's demand-supply gap. Transnational institutions have assisted Malaysia's efforts to establish itself as a regional education hub.

Ziguras, C., L. Reinke, and G. McBurnie. "Hardly Neutral Players: Australia's role in Liberalizing Trade in Education Services." *Globalisation, Societies and Education* 1 no. 3 (2003): 359–74.

Education is a major export for Australia and is viewed as an industry as well as a sector. Unlike the United States and Canada, Australia has pursued expansion of its transnational education services and demonstrated that it considers this sector to be a viable, market-oriented product. The Australian government has changed its education regulations to encourage free trade in education while also assuring that issues such as quality and consumer protection are not ignored.

The Cross-Border Education Research Team (C-BERT) maintains an up-to-date bibliography at www.globalhighered.org. Christine Farrugia led the development of this bibliography, with the support of Jill Borgos, Tom Enderlein, Dan Knox, David Philips, and Linda Tsevi.

INDEX

Abi-Mershed, O., 93
Abu Dhabi, 23, 65, 93
"Academic Building Boom Transforms the Persian Gulf" (*Education Digest*), 93
Academic staff, 19–28; and devolved and less devolved scenarios for quality assurance, 26; and evolving factors in leadership and management, 27–28; and four-way matrix of curriculum development, 25; identifying IBC setting and expectations of, 21–24; level of integration between branch campus and home, 22; managing *versus* leading *versus* administering, 24–25; and perspectives of individual and institution, 26–27; strategies for managing and leading, in multiple countries, 19–28
ACE. *See* American Council on Education (ACE)
Acropolises, 84
"Across the Divide" (*Higher Education Research and Development*), 103
Adams, A. V., 43
Africa, 69
Agricultural and Mechanical College of Texas, 31
Ali al-Thani, Abdulla bin, 31
Aliant International University, 6
Altbach, P. G., 11, 87
Al-Vähälä, T, 61
American Association of Community Colleges, 43
American community college model: and developing and leveraging international partnerships, 44–49; and exportable components, 49–50; international application of, 41–52; and Qatar experience, 47–49; and setting up degree program in Vietnam, 45–47; transported globally, 42–44
American Council on Education (ACE), 61, 89
American Intercontinental University, 6
American Universities on a Global Market, 98
Arab Gulf, resources on, 93–94
Archipelagos, 83–84
ASHE Higher Education Report, 90

Asia, resources on, 94–96
Asia Pacific Education Review, 95–96
Association of European Universities, 61
Association of Universities and Colleges of Canada (AUCC), 61
Aubert, J., 43
AUCC. *See* Association of Universities and Colleges of Canada (AUCC)
AUQA. *See* Australian Universities Quality Agency
Australia, 7, 60, 81, 82, 88, 95, 99, 107
Australian Educational Researcher, 106–107
Australian Journal of Education, 98, 106
Australian Universities, 13
Australian Universities Quality Agency (AUQA), 57–58, 60, 102
Australian University Review, 104–105

Bangladesh, 96
Bartell, M., 29
Bashshur, M., 93
Becker, R., 6, 8, 49, 87–88
Belgium, 6
Bernasconi, A., 41–42, 67, 90
Berniaz, K., 8
Bible, D. X., 35
Blackmur, D., 100
Bodycott, P., 11, 46
Bohm, A., 99
Bologna process, 61
"Borderless Education and Teaching and Learning Cultures" (*Australian University Review*), 104–105
Borneo, 83
Boston University, 6
Brazil/U.S. Exchange Network, 44
Bretag, T., 22, 98
Brimmer, E., 41, 42, 49
Brown, M. C., 90–91
Bryan, Texas, 32
Building Capacity through Cross-Border Tertiary Education (Vincent-Lancrin), 97
Bulgaria, 96

Calderon, L., 89
Campus boundaries, 13

109

110 Multinational Colleges and Universities

Carnegie Mellon University, 2, 30
Carroll, M., 59, 102
"Catch Me I'm Falling" (*Journal of Higher Education Policy and Management*), 98
C-BERT (Cross-Border Education Research Team). *See* Cross-Border Education Research Team (C-BERT)
CCQ. *See* Community College at Qatar (CCQ)
Centro Federal de Educacao Tecnologica (CEFET; Brazil), 44
Chambers, G. S., 6–7
Chan, D., 94
Chapman, D. W., 88, 94–95
CHEA. *See* Council for Higher Education Accreditation (CHEA)
Cheung, P.P.T., 55
China, 21, 57, 83, 88, 89, 94, 95–96, 99–100
Chinese higher education system, 20
Clery Act, 73
Code of Practice for Institutional Audit (Malaysian Qualifications Agency), 60
Code of Practice for the Assurance of Academic Quality and Standards in Higher Education (Quality Assurance Agency for Higher Education), 57
Coleman, D., 13, 66, 100
College of the North Atlantic, Qatar, 30
College Station, Texas, 31, 32, 35
Commonwealth of Learning/Paris (UNESCO), 96–97, 105–106
Community College at Qatar (CCQ), 48–49
"Complexity in Quality Assurance in a Rapidly Growing Free Economic Environment" (*Quality in Higher Education*), 102
Corporate taxes, 72
Council for Higher Education Accreditation (CHEA), 61
"Critical Analysis of the UNESCO/OECD Guidelines for Quality Provision of Cross-Border Higher Education" (*Quality in Higher Education*), 100
Crombie Borgos, J., 1
Croom, P., 88
Crosling, G., 100
Cross Border Collaborations in Higher Education (Chapman and Sakamoto), 94–95
"Crossborder Education" (*Higher Education: Handbook of Theory and Research*), 90
Cross-border education policy context: and acropolises, 84; and archipelagos,

83–84; and educational hubs, 82–83; and emerging policy context, 80–84; and exporting governments, 81–82; and globalization, 80; and importing governments, 82; introduction to, 79–80; and national competitiveness, 81; and national sovereignty, 81; and trade policies, 80–81
Cross-Border Education Research Team (C-BERT), 1, 2, 6, 7, 10, 49, 87
"Cross-Border Higher Education: Issues and Implications for Quality Assurance and Accreditation" (*Higher Education in the World 2007*), 100–101
Cross-Border Partnerships in Higher Education (Chapman and Sakamoto), 88
Cross-Border Tertiary Education (OECD), 97
Cultural impact, 11–12
Cummings, W. K., 6–7
Curriculum development, four-way matrix of, 25
Cyprus, 57

Davis, D., 99
Debowski, S., 9, 11, 103
"Decision Making for Offshore Activities" (*Transnational Education Providers, Partners and Policy*), 99
Department of Foreign Affairs and Trade (Australia), 80
"Developing Transnational Higher Education" (*International Journal of Educational Reform*), 94
Dias, M. A. R., 55
Doha, Qatar, 47–49
Downs, Pinky (coach), 34
Dubai, 8, 10, 15, 58–60, 88, 90, 93, 101; Knowledge and Human Development Authority (KHDA), 59; Knowledge Village, 93
Dubai International Academic City, 84
Dubai School of Government, 101
Dunn, L., 103–104
Dunworth, K., 77, 97–98

EAP. *See* English for Academic Purposes (EAP; University of Nottingham)
Eaton, J. S., 61
Eckel, P. D., 8, 89
"Economic Analysis of Transnational Education" (*Education Economics*), 96
Education Across Borders: Politics, Policy, and Legislative Action (Fegan and Fields), 88

Education City University (ECU; Qatar), 31

Education Economics, 96

"Educational Hubs: Archipelagos & Acropolises" (*International Higher Education*), 89

Educational Technology and Society, 105

"Educational Technology in Transnational Higher Education in Southeast Asia" (*Educational Technology and Society*), 105

Edwards, J., 98, 100

Edwards, R., 98, 100

Egypt, 10–11

Eide, E. R., 48

Employment matters, 74–76

Enderlein, T., 1

English for Academic Purposes (EAP; University of Nottingham), 20

ENQA. *See* European Association for Quality Assurance in Higher Education (ENQA)

Environmental issues, 72

EU. *See* European Union (EU)

European Association for Quality Assurance in Higher Education (ENQA), 61, 62

European Higher Education Area, 62

European Quality Assurance Register for Higher Education, 62

European Union (EU), 72, 74

European University Association, 61, 62

Export control regulations, 73

Exporting governments, 81–82

Farrugia, C., 1

Feast, V., 22, 98

Fegan, J., 9, 82, 88

Field, M. H., 9, 82, 88

Florida State University, 6

Flowers, B. S., 43

Foreign Corrupt Practices Act, 73

"Framework for Sustainability of an Offshore Education Program" (*Journal of International Business and Economics*), 99

France, 15

French Fashion University Esmod, 7

Friedman, T., 5

Fritz, R., 43

Fry, G. W., 45

Garrett, R., 89

GATS. *See* General Agreement on Trade in Services (GATS)

Geloso-Grosso, M., 97

General Agreement on Trade in Services (GATS), 60–61, 80–81, 91, 97, 105–106

Georgetown University, 30

Georgia Institute of Technology, 15

Gill, E. K., 35

Global Alliance for Transnational Education, 61

"Global Assemblage" (*World Development*), 96

"Global Growth of Private Higher Education" (*ASHE Higher Education Report*), 90

Global University Network for Innovation, 100–101

Globalisation, Societies and Education 1, 107

Globalization, 80

Globalization and the Market in Higher Education (Uvalic-Trumbic), 95

Goldblatt, D., 80

Greece, 6, 57, 106

Green, M., 8, 89

Gribble, K., 104

Guidelines for Quality Provision in Cross Border Higher Education (UNESCO), 62, 102

Hall, J. E., 30, 98

Harding, M., 3, 65

"Hardly Neutral Players" (Globalisation, Societies and Education 1), 107

Harrington, C., 28

Harvey, L., 54

HCC. *See* Houston Community College (HCC)

Hefferman, T., 13, 98

Held, D., 80

Higher Education, Free Zones, and Quality Assurance in Dubai (Dubai School of Government), 101

Higher Education Crossing Borders (Commonwealth of Learning/Paris; UNESCO), 105–106

Higher Education: Handbook of Theory and Research (Smart), 90

"Higher Education in the United Emirates" (*Journal of Higher Education Policy and Management*), 93–94

Higher Education in the World 2007 (Global University Network for Innovation), 100–101

Higher Education Policy, 91

Higher Education Research and Development, 98, 103, 104

Hill, B. A., 55

112 MULTINATIONAL COLLEGES AND UNIVERSITIES

Ho Chi Minh City, 45, 96
Holsworth, R. D., 8
Home country, 5
Home-country compliance, 72–73
Hong Kong, 57, 94
Hopper, R., 97
Horizontal boundaries, 13
Hosie, P., 82
Host country, 5
Houston, Texas, 43; Vietnamese community in, 45
Houston Community College (HCC), 3, 30, 42–50
Howman, C., 3
Huang, F., 94
Hughes, R., 2–3, 19
Huisman, J., 103
Hussin, V., 104

IAU. *See* International Association of Universities (IAU)
IBCs. *See* International branch campuses (IBCs)
"Ideas and Realities" (*Quality in Higher Education*), 97–98
IIE Network, 43
"Impact of the GATS on Transnational Tertiary Education" (*Australian Educational Researcher*), 106–107
Importing governments, 82
"Importing Private Higher Education" (*Journal of Comparative Policy Analysis*), 90
Incheon, South Korea, 84
India, 57, 81, 89
Indonesia, 97
Innovations in Education and Teaching International, 104
Institutional ethos: and altering traditions and preserving values, 35–36; and Qatar Education City, 30–31; and replicating student experience, 29–39; and replicating traditions, 33–35; and respecting cultural conflicts, 36–37
Instituto Federal do Espirito Santo (IFES; Brazil), 44
Instituto Federal Fluminense (IFF; Brazil), 44
Insurance, 72
International Association of Universities (IAU), 61, 91
International branch campuses (IBCs), 1–4, 7; applying American community college model to, 41–52; and campus boundaries, 13; and challenges of spanning boundaries, 12–14; cultural impact of, 11–12; and development of research capacity, 15; global growth of, 6–7; and horizontal boundaries, 13; interaction of, with local environment, 9–12; managerial and leadership challenges in global expansion of, 5–16; and managing and leading academic staff in multiple countries, 19–28; and need for comparative data, 14; number of, by geographic location, 7; public diplomacy role of, 15; purposes and roles of (2010), 7–8; and temporal boundaries, 13–14
International branch campuses, operational considerations for, 65–78; and employment matters, 74–76; and home-country compliance, 72–73; and initial challenges and considerations, 66–67; and ongoing back-office support, 76; and partnering with local institutions, 77; and planning in foreign country, 70–71; and policies and ongoing governance, 69–70; and regulatory matters, 72; and understanding local laws, 67–69
International Branch Campuses: Markets and Strategies (Becker), 87–88
International Branch Campuses: Scale and Significance (Garrett), 89
International Branch Campus-Models and Trends (Verbik and Merkley), 92–93
International Center for Education, Language, and Technology (ICELT; Brazil), 44
International Education, 105
International Higher Education, 87, 89, 91, 95
International Journal of Educational Reform, 94
"International Linkages in Malaysian Private Higher Education" (*International Higher Education*), 95
International Network for Quality Assurance Agencies in Higher Education (INQAAHE), 62
"International Partnerships: A Game Theory Perspective" (*New Directions for Higher Education*), 99
International University Vietnam (RMIT; Royal Melbourne Institute of Technology), 96
Internationalisation and Trade in Higher Education (OECD), 106
"Internationalism of Education" (*Australian Journal of Education*), 98

"Internationalization of Higher Education in the Developing and Emerging Countries" (*Journal of Studies in International Education*), 94
Ireland, 88
IRS Form 990, 73
Iskander, Malaysia, 84
Islamic cultures, 11
Italy, 6

Jackson, S., 57
Jakarta, Indonesia, 100
Jamaica, 96
Japan, 6–7, 88, 94, 106
Jaworski, J., 43
Johns Hopkins University, 6
"Joint Ventures in Cross-Border Higher Education" (*Cross Border Collaborations in Higher Education*), 94–95
Jokivirta, L., 106
Journal of Comparative Policy Analysis, 90
Journal of Higher Education Policy and Management, 93–94, 98, 100
Journal of International Business and Economics, 99
Journal of Studies in International Education, 94, 96, 100, 103

Kamlet, M., 2
Kelley, M. E., 104–105
Khalifa al-Thani, Hamad bin, 30
Kim, E. H., 98
King Saud University/Riyadh Community College (RCC), 44
Kinser, K., 1, 3, 8, 9, 41–42, 47, 53, 55, 56, 58, 63, 67, 79, 81–83, 89–91
Knight, J., 82–83, 90, 97, 100–101, 105–106
Knox, D., 1, 81–82
Krieger, Z., 93
Kristoffersen, D., 58
Kuala Lampur, Malaysia, 83, 100
Kuh, G. D., 29–30

Lammey, R. W., 3, 65
Lane, J. E., 1–3, 5, 8–10, 13, 41–42, 47, 58–59, 66, 77, 79, 81–83, 89, 90–91, 94–95, 101
Latin America, 88
"Learning to Teach Offshore" (*Higher Education Research and Development*), 104
Lee, M., 82, 95
Levy, D. A., 8, 90
Levy, D. C., 41–42, 58, 67, 90
Lewis, R., 54

"Liberal Arts Education in Qatar" (*International Education*), 105
Lien, D., 96
Lim, F.C.B., 13, 101
Local laws, understanding, 67–69
Luu, D. T., 89

Malaysia, 8, 15, 20, 57, 83, 90, 91, 95, 96, 100, 101, 106–107
Malaysian Qualifications Agency (MQA), 59, 60
Martin, M., 54, 55
Martorell, F., 48
Mauritius, 97
Mazzarol, T., 82
McBurnie, G., 1, 8, 11, 27–28, 55, 65, 67, 82, 91–92, 95, 99, 106, 107
McGrew, D., 80
Merkley, C., 6, 8, 92–93
Mexico, 6
Middle East, 9, 12, 13, 15, 29, 43, 47, 69
Middle East North African (MENA) countries, 43
Middlehurst, R., 96–97
Middlesex University (United Kingdom), 15
Ministry of Trade and Industry (MTI; Singapore), 80
Mok, K. H., 95–96
Monash University, 99
Morrill Land Grant Act (1862), 31–32
"Motivations and Aspirations for International Branch Campuses" (*Cross-Border Collaborations in Higher Education*), 88
MQA. *See* Malaysian Qualifications Agency (MQA)
MTI. *See* Ministry of Trade and Industry (MTI; Singapore)
Muslim countries, 13–14
Muslim culture, 11–12, 34

Naidoo, V., 8, 65, 92
NASA, 43
Nasser al-Misnad, Mozah, 31, 48
National Cancer Center (Malaysia), 15
National competitiveness, 81
National Regulatory Frameworks for Transnational Higher Education (Observatory on Borderless Education), 106
National sovereignty, 81
New Directions for Higher Education, 99
New York University (NYU), 22, 65, 69; Abu Chabi campus, 65, 69

114 MULTINATIONAL COLLEGES AND UNIVERSITIES

Ng, P. T., 94
Ningbo, China, 20
Northwestern University, 30
Norway, 7
Nye, J., 81
NYU. *See* New York University (NYU)

"Observations from the Edge of the Deluge" *(Trajectories of Education in the Arab World)*, 93
Observatory on Borderless Higher Education (London), 87–89, 92–93, 97, 106
OECD, 97, 102, 106
Office of Foreign Asset Control (OFAC), 73
Olds, K., 96
Olsen, A., 99
On the Ground Overseas (Green, Kinser, and Eckel), 89
Open Doors (IIE Network), 43
Otieno, W., 41–42, 67, 90
"Outsourcing University Degrees" *(Journal of Higher Education Policy and Management)*, 100

Palgrave Prize in Higher Education Policy Research (International Association of Universities; 2010), 91
Panama Canal Zone, 6
Pascarella, E. T., 30
Pearcey, M. A., 90–91
Perraton, J., 80
Persian Gulf, 92–93
Phillips, D., 1
Pollock, A., 99
Poole, D., 13, 98
Portal system, 22
Portugal, 88
Principles of Good Practice in Overseas International Education Programs for Non-U.S. Nationals, 56
Private Higher Education Institution Act (1996; Malaysia), 106–107
"Private Nature of Cross-Border Higher Education" *(International Higher Education)*, 91

QAA. *See* Quality Assurance Agency for Higher Education (QAA)
Qatar, 88, 91, 93, 105
Qatar, State of, 11, 29, 30, 35, 42, 47–49
Qatar Education City, 30–31, 35, 47, 84, 93
Qatar Foundation, 30–32, 37–38, 47, 84

Qatar University, 48
Qatari Supreme Education Council (SEC), 48
Quality assurance, multinational, 53–64; and Australia, 57–58; and definition of quality assurance, 54–55; devolved and less devolved scenarios for, 26; and Dubai, 58–59; external, 55–60; and Malaysia, 59–60; and United Kingdom, 56–57; and United States, 55–59
Quality Assurance Agency for Higher Education (QAA), 56–57, 60, 63
Quality Assurance in Education, 101–102
"Quality Assurance in Transnational Education" *(Journal of Studies in International Education)*, 100
Quality in Higher Education, 97, 100, 102
"Quality of Transnational Education: A Provider View" *(Quality in Higher Education)*, 102

Ramadan, 12
Rawazik, W., 59, 102
"Reconsidering Privatization in Cross-Border Engagements" *(Higher Education Policy)*, 91
Regulatory matters, 72
Reiffers, J., 43
Reinke, L., 107
"Remaking the World in Our Own Image" *(Australian Journal of Education)*, 106
Report of Foreign Bank and Financial Accounts (FBAR), 73
"Responding to Crises in Transnational Education" *(Higher Education Research and Development)*, 98
Restriction of Hazardous Substances (RoHS) directives, 72
Reveille (mascot), 37
Rizvi, F., 8
RMIT. *See* Royal Melbourne Institute of Technology (RMIT)
"RMIT Vietnam and Vietnam's Development" *(Journal of Studies in International Education)*, 96
Role of Transnational, Private, and For-Profit Provision in Meeting Global Demand for Tertiary Education (Middlehurst and Woodfield), 96–97
Rostron, M., 11, 47, 105
Royal Melbourne Institute of Technology (RMIT), 96

Saarinen, T., 61
Saigon Institute of Information Technology, 45
Saigon Tech, 45–48
Sakamoto, R., 88, 94–95
Sanyal, B. C., 54, 55
Sarawak, 91
SARS epidemic, 98
Saudi Arabia, 93
Scharmer, C. O., 43
Schibik, T., 28
Scott, W. R., 12
Selvarajah, C., 9, 99
Senge, P. M., 43
"Sharing Quality Higher Education Across Borders" (CHEA, IAU, AUCC, ACE), 61
Silas Casillas, J. C., 41–42, 67, 90
Singapore, 83, 89, 94, 96
Slantcheva-Durst, S., 41–42, 67, 90
Smart, J. C., 90
South Africa, 83, 88, 106
South Korea, 83
Southeast Asia, 13, 69
Southern Association of Colleges and Schools (SACS), 45
Spangler, M. S., 3, 41
"Spirit of Aggieland," 33
Stakeholder theory, 99
Stasz, C., 48
State University of New York, Albany, 1, 6
Stenden University, 30
"Student Recruitment at International Branch Campuses" (*Journal of Studies in International Education*), 103
"Supporting Off-Shore Students" (*Innovations in Education and Teaching International*), 104
Switzerland, 6

Tak, S. H., 104–105
Tashkent, 22
Tax requirements, 73
Teaching in Transnational Higher Education (Dunn and Wallace), 103–104
Temple University, 6
Temporal boundaries, 13–14
Terenzini, P. T., 30
Tertiary Education Quality and Standards Agency (TEQSA), 58
Texas A&M University, Qatar (TAMQ), 3, 11, 29–39; altering traditions and preserving values at, 35–36; development of, 31–33; lessons learned from,
37–39; and replicating traditions, 33–35; and respecting cultural conflicts, 36–37; and Texas A&M traditions in Qatar, 33–37
Texas A&M University Traditions Council, 36
Texas Medical Center Methodist Hospital, 47
Tierney, W. G., 29
Trade policies, 80–81
Trajectories of Education in the Arab World (Abi-Mershed), 93
Trani, E. P., 8
"Transnational Campuses" (Lane, Brown, and Pearcey), 90–91
"Transnational Education, Quality, and the Public Good" (*Globalization and the Market in Higher Education*), 95
Transnational Education: Issues and Trends in Offshore Higher Education (McBurnie and Ziguras), 91–92
Transnational Education Providers, Partners and Policy (Davis, Olsen, and Bohm), 99
"Transnational Higher Education: A Stock Taking of Current Activity" (*Journal of Studies in International Education*), 92
"Transnational Higher Education: Why It Happens and Who Benefits" (*International Higher Education*), 92
Tsevi, L., 1
Tyler, A. Q., Jr., 3, 41

"Understanding Quality Assurance: A Cross Country Case Study" (*Quality Assurance in Education*), 101
UNESCO, 55, 61–62, 95, 100, 102, 105–106; Education for All campaign, 42
"Unique Campus Contexts" (*New Directions for Institutional Research*), 90–91
United Arab Emirates, 7, 29, 59, 65, 81, 93–94
United Kingdom, 6, 7, 21, 81, 82, 88, 103
United Nations, 81
United States, 7, 81
"Universities as Firms" (*American Universities on a Global Market*), 98–99
Universities UK, 56
University, 21
University at Albany, State University of New York, 1, 6
University of Calgary, Qatar, 30

University of La Verne (United States), 6
University of Nebraska, 34
University of Nottingham (United Kingdom), 3, 15, 21; English for Academic Purposes (EAP), 20
University of Sheffield (United Kingdom), 2–3
University of Wollongong-Dubai (UOWD; Australia), 15
University Quality Assurance International Board (UQAIB), 59, 63
Uppsala model, 98
UQAIB. *See* University Quality Assurance International Board (UQAIB)
US Bureau of Economic Analysis (BEA), 80
USAID/Higher Education Development grant, 44
Uvalic-Trumbic, S., 53, 54, 61–63, 95
Uzbeck, 22

Value-added tax (VAT), 72
van Ginkel, H. J. A., 55
Venturing Abroad (Green and Eckel), 89
Verbik, L., 6, 8, 92–93, 106
Vietnam, 42, 49, 83, 94, 96, 99; Consul General, 46; setting up degree program in, 45–47
Vietnam War, 46
Vincent-Lancrin, S., 97
Vinen, D. G., 9, 99
Virginia Commonwealth University, 30
Walker, A., 11, 47
Wallace, M., 103–104

Waste Electrical and Electronic Equipment (WEEE), 72
Webster University (United States), 6
Weill Cornell Medical College, 30
Westminster International University, Tashkent (WIUT), 22
Westminster University (United Kingdom), 22
"When China Opens to the World" (*Asia Pacific Education Review*), 95–96
"Why Branch Campuses May Be Unsustainable" (*International Higher Education*), 87
Wildavsky, B., 23, 82
Wilkins, S., 93–94, 103
Wilmoth, D., 96
WIUT. *See* Westminster International University, Tashkent (WIUT)
Wood, C. H., 11, 29
Woodfield, S., 96–97
Woodhouse, D., 58, 102
World Development, 96
World Is Flat, The (Friedman), 5
World Trade Organization (WTO), 80

Xu, X., 95–96

Yale University, 23
Yiyun, J., 99–100

Zhu, M., 98
Ziguras, C, 1, 8, 11, 27–28, 55, 65, 67, 77, 82, 91–92, 104–107

NEW DIRECTIONS FOR HIGHER EDUCATION

ORDER FORM SUBSCRIPTION AND SINGLE ISSUES

DISCOUNTED BACK ISSUES:

Use this form to receive 20% off all back issues of *New Directions for Higher Education*.
All single issues priced at **$23.20** (normally $29.00)

TITLE	ISSUE NO.	ISBN

Call 888-378-2537 or see mailing instructions below. When calling, mention the promotional code JBNND
to receive your discount. For a complete list of issues, please visit www.josseybass.com/go/ndhe

SUBSCRIPTIONS: (1 YEAR, 4 ISSUES)

☐ New Order ☐ Renewal

U.S.	☐ Individual: $89	☐ Institutional: $259
CANADA/MEXICO	☐ Individual: $89	☐ Institutional: $299
ALL OTHERS	☐ Individual: $113	☐ Institutional: $333

Call 888-378-2537 or see mailing and pricing instructions below.
Online subscriptions are available at www.onlinelibrary.wiley.com

ORDER TOTALS:

Issue / Subscription Amount: $ _____

Shipping Amount: $ _____
(for single issues only – subscription prices include shipping)

Total Amount: $ _____

SHIPPING CHARGES:

First Item	$5.00
Each Add'l Item	$3.00

(No sales tax for U.S. subscriptions. Canadian residents, add GST for subscription orders. Individual rate subscriptions must
be paid by personal check or credit card. Individual rate subscriptions may not be resold as library copies.)

BILLING & SHIPPING INFORMATION:

☐ **PAYMENT ENCLOSED:** *(U.S. check or money order only. All payments must be in U.S. dollars.)*

☐ **CREDIT CARD:** ☐ VISA ☐ MC ☐ AMEX

Card number _____ Exp. Date _____

Card Holder Name _____ Card Issue # _____

Signature _____ Day Phone _____

☐ **BILL ME:** *(U.S. institutional orders only. Purchase order required.)*

Purchase order # _____
Federal Tax ID 13559302 • GST 89102-8052

Name _____

Address _____

Phone _____ E-mail _____

Copy or detach page and send to: **John Wiley & Sons, PTSC, 5th Floor**
989 Market Street, San Francisco, CA 94103-1741

Order Form can also be faxed to: **888-481-2665**

PROMO JBNND